Three Ways to Fail

CONTEMPORARY ETHNOGRAPHY

Series Editor:
Alma Gottlieb

A complete list of books in this series
is available from the publisher.

THREE WAYS TO FAIL

Journeys Through Mapuche Chile

Magnus Course

PENN

UNIVERSITY OF PENNSYLVANIA PRESS

PHILADELPHIA

Published by
University of Pennsylvania Press
Philadelphia, Pennsylvania 19104-4112
www.pennpress.org

Printed in the United States of America on acid-free paper
10 9 8 7 6 5 4 3 2 1

Paperback ISBN: 978-1-5128-2656-2
Hardcover ISBN: 978-1-5128-2655-5
eBook ISBN: 978-1-5128-2657-9

A Cataloging-in-Publication record is
available from the Library of Congress

To two wonderful teachers:
Sergio Hernán Painemilla Huarapil
&
the late Peter George Gow

Contents

Preface

I sit by a tree at the edge of a lake. It's the same tree I sat by twenty-five years ago, in what seems to me now to have been a different life, a different world. I stare east across the lake, and the world appears to me as lines, straight lines: the upright reeds, the raised path to the island, the distant horizon. The Mapuche people with whom I lived all those years ago taught me that a person must strive to be *norche*, a "direct person," as clear, simple, and straight as the flight lines of the black-necked swans that fill the lake. They frequently fail at this, as do I—as do we all. Yet the people here allow the world around them to guide them toward a wisdom that ushers us gently back to a better way of living, a better way of participating in the endless flow of life.

The stories that make up this book are the story of how my lived engagement with this wisdom taught me both how to recognize the nature of my failures and how to grow beyond them. So I return to this tree—a *folo* tree that stands alone at the lake's side; old, yet small, with dark, pungent, glossy leaves that Marta uses to make tea—and I pick myself up from failure and start again.

* * *

The Mapuche people have cared for and shaped the landscapes of southern Chile and Argentina for many centuries and have continued that care in the face of a brutal and avaricious colonialism. Yet this book about how to live better is not simply a romanticized portrait of a people living "at one" with their environment and each other. It is, rather, a set of reflections about my own journey through three distinct Mapuche archetypes—namely the witch, the clown, and the usurper—of how people *fail* to live with their environment and with each other, and about the relevance that this journey has had for me in trying to move beyond my own shortcomings. I have learned that these archetypes can be inhabited by any of us, male or female, old or young, rich or poor. Usually, when people appropriate from other cultures, they steal the good stuff; here I find myself stealing the bad, not through any morbid, voyeuristic fascination with the dark underbelly of Mapuche life but rather because, as with a photographic negative, it's these very archetypes of failure that make the key attributes of a good life clear, through their absence, their negation, and their denial. The failures of the witch, the clown, and the usurper, each in their own way, make clear what it means to live well, to be a true person: *kümeche* (generous), *norche* (direct), *kimche* (wise), and *newenche* (strong).

∗ ∗ ∗

Southern Chile on a windswept winter's morning can be described as neither shimmering nor colorful, unless one looks too closely at the spilled diesel refracting in the muddy puddles of the port's main street. The pervasive gray I found when I first descended from the bus all those years ago seemed to match and exceed the gray I thought I'd left behind. Gray skies, gray houses, gray trees, and endless stretches of gray-green gorse withering back from the ocean's relentless wind. It was the continual roar of the Pacific that first reinforced for me that I wasn't at home, an omnipresent grumbling and growling to the west as huge breakers hurled themselves into the land. A slow, meandering gravel road connects the small port to the various communities around the lake some fifteen miles to the south. The lake itself lies amid low hills that stretch right up to the great ocean, the *füta lafken*, with only a narrow isthmus of land separating it from the sea's salty waters. In fact, so frequently do ocean storms breach the isthmus at its narrowest point that the lake's waters are brackish, not sweet.

This is Mapuche territory. Nearly all of the people whose scattered homesteads dot the hills and gullies that cover this area are Mapuche, an Indigenous people whose territory once covered almost the entirety of South America's Southern Cone, from the Pacific to the Atlantic. Defeat by the Chilean and Argentine armies at the end of the nineteenth century led to the Mapuche people's confinement on small reservations, which constituted but a fraction of their former lands. Over the course of the twentieth century and into the twenty-first, these lands have been further depleted by a continual process of usurpation by timber and cattle interests, a process only made possible through the tacit support of the Chilean state. In recent years, the Mapuche people's struggle to regain their stolen land and assert their rights to self-determination and autonomy has faced increasingly violent repression, a conflict I return to later in this book. Back then, the people I knew around the lake made a living through a mixture of subsistence farming, mainly wheat and potatoes, and a variety of government subsidies that barely held the worst ravages of poverty at bay. It was these people who showed me—despite the turmoil, tragedy, and injustice of their lives—what it meant to be truly *che*, a "true person."

I first came to the lake more than two decades ago, largely by chance. The first years I spent there, I was working for a small Chilean organization that designed and implemented programs for bilingual education comprising both Spanish and the Mapuche language, Mapudungun. Then, after a yearlong pause back home in Britain, I returned to live at the lake to carry out the research for a doctorate in anthropology. And after the doctorate was completed, I returned to the lake yet again for another year of research, this time focused on the shifting politics of language. I've returned to the lake for short visits every couple of years during the past two decades, but the period I speak of in this book refers mainly to the couple of years before and the couple of years after the turn of the new millennium. All told, I spent just shy of five years at the lake. I was young then, a youth truly alone for the first time, still to recognize either the cruelty of the world or its providence. That the people of the lake took me in amazes me still, and their love and kindness toward me constitutes the background against which the failures I recount in these pages stand out.

*   *   *

In recent years, an entire self-help industry has evolved to exhort us to grow through our failures, to learn from our mistakes, each failure simply a minor diversion on the pathway to achievement. We're often presented with an array of carefully manicured and curated failures that point the way to the rehabilitation of our shortcomings, as we become ever more self-realized. There is clearly a degree of truth in this characterization: we can learn from our mistakes, and we can indeed grow through our failures. Yet many of us find that although we *can* learn and grow, we frequently *don't*. Like an errant child banging its head against the wall, we repeat the same mistake again and again and again. We find that our failure is thus double: first we fail, and then we fail to redeem that failure into something positive. We fail at failing. We have perhaps lost the freedom to truly fail. We're also frequently left wondering: What actually constitutes failure? Who gets to decide? And perhaps more importantly: What exactly is it that failure fails to achieve? What is its opposite? We might answer "success," but that would simply defer the deeper question of how we should live, what kind of people we actually want to be.

   An alternative approach can be found when we explore how different societies in different parts of the world engage with failure, an exploration that reveals that they frequently do so in quite different terms. New doors are opened and new possibilities uncovered and, I would suggest, a more constructive and complete view emerges both of failure and of the alternatives we should be striving for. As this book traces, Mapuche thought on failure offers a positive way forward toward a better way of living, not as some internal project of individual self-realization but rather as, firstly, a kind of moral commentary on the specific kinds of relationships that certain kinds of failure deny and, secondly, an understanding that these failures are not idiosyncratic, individual aberrations but rather intrinsic potentials that reside within us all. It is anthropology—the exploration of social relationships in all of their glorious diversity—that can offer up this comparative perspective, but anthropology also has its own deeply complex, uncomfortable, and far-from-innocent relationship with both failure and the cross-cultural comparisons that allow it to be revealed.

Anthropology is a profession that takes failure in its stride, even makes a virtue of it. Failure, in fact, could be said to be the anthropologist's primary methodology in trying to make sense of the world's near-infinite cultural and social diversity. In the years each anthropologist spends sharing the lives of the people about whom they write—the disciplinary rite of passage known as "fieldwork"—the failures offer an opportunity. Through the inevitable muddling of linguistic meanings, through breaching unspoken social contracts, crashing clumsily through cultural taboos, and failing to ever get the jokes, the anthropologist can slowly and incrementally piece back together the social whole that their failures have shattered. The linguistic meanings become clear, the social contracts explicit, the taboos visible, and the jokes, finally, funny. Like a bat depicting the world around it in stark relief by emitting sounds, anthropologists elicit the world around them through an endless series of failures. Yet while anthropology celebrates failure, it does so only to a point. Eventually the debt must be called in and the failures salvaged, redeemed, and transformed into the completion of a coherent analysis. The anthropologist's failures are thus ultimately placed into a narrative of heroic success. Indeed, the great critic Susan Sontag famously described "the anthropologist as hero" in her review of the French anthropologist Claude Lévi-Strauss's memoir, *Tristes Tropiques*. According to Sontag, the anthropologist is the hero of the modern age due to the pervasive feeling of "homeless-ness" at the heart of Western society: the sheer pace of technological and social change has uprooted us and "led every sensitive modern mind to the recording of some kind of nausea, of intellectual vertigo." The anthropologist is the hero who seeks out an antidote to this mod-ern malaise in implicitly premodern worlds, the places where life can once again be made sense of, its certainties laid bare. The failures of the anthropologist are thus made right through the redemption their sacrifice achieves for Western modernity as a whole.

At the heart of the methodology of failure described above there frequently lies an almost unspoken difference: an understanding that the line between the anthropologist and the people with whom they live corresponds neatly to a predefined and predetermined "us" and "them." Were the anthropologist to fail in their own society, their fail-ures would surely be nothing other than, well, failures. They would be generative of nothing other than a sense of embarrassment and disappointment. There would seem to be nothing particularly heroic about studying oneself. And on the scale of the discipline writ large, where would anthropology be if it were to abandon its adventures into the exotic unknown, to seek an antidote to the ills of Western modernity without leaving that self-same modernity behind? Son-tag was writing in 1963, and the ironic tone of much of her review suggests that even then she was more than aware that the certainties of the boundary between a Western "us" and a non-Western "them" were already crumbling, both politically and intellectually, and that, in fact, this boundary had been nothing more than a superficial con-ceit to begin with.

Not only did anthropology change but so, too, did the way in which it understood itself. The growing number of anthropologists from outside the West, combined with increased anthropological interest in Western society itself, made the conventional boundary between "them" and "us" problematic to say the least. And this wasn't simply a problem of methods, but a problem also of both ethics and politics. Who were anthropologists to speak for others? Didn't their analyses and descriptions always transform the fluidity of living, breathing, fighting societies into static textual objects? And why did the flow of anthropologists seem to be all one way, always from the richer North to the poorer South? How could a discipline that so closely resembled the colonial enterprise still flourish in a postcolonial age? In response, the discipline sought to reimagine itself, to repurpose itself as a bastion of liberal values in an increasingly unequal world, as if siding with the underdog would somehow obscure the murkiness at its core.

Yet despite this seismic shift in the way anthropology conceived of itself, and despite the ubiquity of a new politics of representation, the basic structure of the anthropological enterprise has remained relatively unchanged. Like smokers faced with images of cancer-ridden organs on the sides of their cigarette packs, anthropologists see the violence of their ethnographic representations and go ahead and do it anyway. You could describe this as the failure of anthropology, and there is no end of self-flagellation at a collective disciplinary level—panels at conferences, opinion pieces in leading journals, lectures to students—all decrying the discipline's role in reproducing the world's inequalities. What is much, much rarer is the taking of personal responsibility at an individual level, for even anthropology's harshest critics rarely show even the least degree of self-incrimination for their own part in the discipline's failings. To locate failure at the abstract level of a global academic discipline actually serves to shield anthropologists from thinking too closely about their own failures: not those analytically productive failures of crossed communications or defamed taboos but the deeper, somewhat darker failures, failures that are failures no matter where or by whom they are committed.

In this book I try, as much as I can, not to shy away from my various failures, not to simply project them onto the anthropological

project of which I was once a part. It would be an overstatement, I
think, to say that anthropology has been a complete failure; we know
so much more about the world because of it, about the myriad forms
of human potentiality, about the countless ways that the injustice and
inequality that hamper that potential reemerge. But this is not to say
that the project doesn't need to be reconsidered. As I will suggest,
the anthropology that I knew, and in which I enthusiastically par-
ticipated for decades, has to be given up. Given up not in the sense
of being ceased or abandoned but in the sense of being handed over
to others, returned to others. But first, having taken this brief diversion to explore the failure of anthropology itself, let me return to the
Mapuche thinking on failure that anthropology reveals.

*   *   *

In the stories that follow, I reflect upon my own failures and the failures of others, as we fall into the archetypes of witch, clown, and
usurper through which Mapuche thought on failure becomes most
apparent. As mentioned above, such archetypes don't present failure
as a step on the road to some process of personal growth or self-
realization; they take a different tack. Mapuche failure is frequently
an end point, a cul-de-sac from which there is no return. The failures
of the witch, the clown, and the usurper ultimately end in death, an
irreconcilable, irredeemable death. Their failings are an intrinsic part
of what and who they are: if a witch did not destroy, they would not
be a witch; if a clown did not confuse the boundaries of desire, they
would not be a clown; if a usurper did not seek to possess, they would
not be a true usurper at all. Such figures neither learn nor grow from
their failures but repeat them ad infinitum, turning farce inevitably
into tragedy. These caricatures of failure exist both as personified by
specific individuals but also, and perhaps more importantly, as capac-
ities that exist within us all. Their embodiment in specific people
makes the witch, the clown, and the usurper into tangible figures,

known and real, rather than abstract instances of unmoored values. Yet it is our own capacity to slip into these caricatures that makes them frightening: the fact that the failures they exemplify already dwell within us all.

Some of the older Mapuche people I know still tell the old tales, the stories of *Ngürü*, Fox. Fox not only fails, he fails spectacularly: he gets his mouth sewn shut by Partridge, and then he gets eaten by Puma. And even his successes consist of the dramatic failures of others: he tricks Puma into eating her own cubs, and then fools her into getting crushed by an avalanche. The stories of tricksters like Fox reverberate and refract all around the Americas and far beyond, stories of the genius fool who despite his cunning and intelligence fails to ever really see what life is truly about. These stories are entertainment, but they are also far more than that; like the figures of the witch, the clown, and the usurper, they shed light on the various forms that failure can take; on how greed, destruction, and dishonesty can lead to our demise. And I would contend that thinking about failures—our own and those of others—can give us a little clarity on the human condition. Through reflecting on these stories and archetypes of failure, we start to recognize what our actions really are, to see what potentials are emerging within us, and to avoid simply looking to others as the sole cause of our woes. For if there's one thing people do, it is to fail, and reflecting on failure allows us to see that, not only in others' behavior but in our own; we recognize ourselves as fellow members of the global congregation of the failed, and this recognition gives us a surer footing from which to take life up again.

*   *   *

The first time I met Esteban, he looked like he was about to blow away. He was a very slight, slim man whose shirt and trousers whipped around his body in the fierce southern wind. His shoes were polished, but he wore no socks, and his pale brown eyes danced with light and laughter. He had a surprisingly red mustache, the source of his nickname, *Kelüpayun*, "Redbeard" in Mapudungun, the Mapuche language. Esteban was, at that time, president of his community and also one of the leaders of an association that sought to bring together the various Mapuche communities dotted around the lake. I got to know Esteban over repeated visits to the lake, and eventually he suggested that rather than wasting a large chunk of each day on the cramped bus that ran between the regional capital and the port, I could move in with him and experience life at the lake firsthand. And for the next couple of years, while I lived with Esteban and his family in their homestead, he often talked of politics, of racism, and of the discrimination he'd faced while living far to the north in Santiago, during his time as a union organizer, an activity that led to his rapid return south following General Pinochet's 1973 military coup and the years of repression that followed. I have to admit that, to my shame now, I never paid much attention to Esteban's political tribulations. My interest was always in his deep knowledge of Mapuche culture and history and, in particular, of the natural world; we'd go off on long walks or on horseback, recording the names of every plant and every bird we came across. His wife, Florencia, meanwhile, was quiet and reserved, her life dedicated to her children and grandchildren and to maintaining her home as an oasis of tranquility amid the various whirlwinds of Mapuche life.

Eventually, Esteban's children moved back home from the various schools they had been attending, and it was time for me to vacate their spare room, where I had lived amid the sacks filled with wheat and potatoes, and move on. I ended up moving in with Juan and Marta and their five children. They lived just across a heavily wooded gully from Esteban and Florencia, and I already knew their home well, as Juan was Esteban's nephew. Like his uncle, Juan had spent time in Santiago, but never really acclimatized to urban life and soon moved back to the lake. By then in his thirties, he decided it was time to marry, and headed off from the isthmus to the island. The island is indeed an island, but the portion of lake that separates it from the isthmus is so filled with dense reedbeds that sometimes it doesn't much look like one. A raised pathway allows people to cross from the isthmus to the island, although in winter this passage involves going up to one's waist in the lake's icy waters. Juan had crossed the lake and somehow persuaded Marta to marry him, despite barely knowing him. She had clearly been as keen to leave home as I had. A passionate and powerful woman, she would not hesitate to respond to an out-of-place remark with a ferocious severity that could send everybody scurrying. Marta's and Juan's five children were my frequent companions as, like a child myself, I wandered the land with no clear intent, blundering and flailing from one failure to the next. Both Juan and Esteban belonged to a large extended family that occupied all of the homesteads in that particular community. Esteban's many brothers were my "uncles" and would always refer to me with the reciprocal term *malle*, meaning either "nephew" or "uncle." It was to this place and to these people that I belonged, and despite my wanderings over the entire region surrounding the lake, it was to them that I would always return, to them that I was indebted.

*   *   *

Perhaps all my talk of humans as failed beings is slipping too much into a view of the world that is foreign to Mapuche thinking, a view of the world that, either implicitly or explicitly, reflects a biblical notion of original sin, of humans as always being in need of some kind of redemption. One bright spring day, during a pause from plowing what would within months be a field of golden wheat, Esteban explained to me that the Bavarian Capuchin missionaries who arrived at the lake at the turn of the twentieth century translated the Mapuche verb *yafkan* as "to sin." *Sin*—it would be hard to imagine a term with more theological, ontological, and moral baggage than that. But, as Esteban explained, *yafkan* doesn't really mean "to sin" at all, it means simply "to make a mistake." "All people make mistakes, but not all people sin," he told me. "So what's the difference?" I asked. "What would I know? You'll have to ask a sinner that!" he replied, laughing. In some ways, this book is the process of me asking myself that same question. For me at least, the value of reflecting on failure has been primarily neither growth, nor knowledge as such, but clarity. We may not change our ways, we may not redeem ourselves; most likely we will keep banging our heads relentlessly against the same walls, but we will do it with our eyes wide open.

*   *   *

While all of what follows is true, names and places have been changed.

Three Ways to Fail

i

witch

Who is the witch? The witch is the one who destroys. The witch is the one who turns your dreams dark; who buries eggs in the corners of your fields; who sends the creatures that wander through the night; who rattles across your roof hiding unnamed things; who smiles at you kindly as they poison your wine. Why do they do it? Because that is what they do.

Our lives are full of witches. They use the grooves worn by our goodwill, our generosity, our friendship, our love for others, and invert them, turning the gift into a curse, love into hate, care into destruction. The witch watches. They watch us at our birth, they wait, they follow us to the city, they bide their time. They are the harbingers of death to this world. The old people say that without witches there would be no death; we would live to a hundred years, two hundred, maybe more. Mapuche people call them *kalku* and see them all around. They are both men and women, both old and young: our neighbors, our cousins, our colleagues, and our friends.

We recognize the witch in others—name them, blame them, accuse them, pursue them—so as not to recognize the witch in ourselves. When the child lashes out, when the voice is suddenly raised and the bottled smashed into a thousand shards, that is the witch. To imagine terrible hurt descending on those who have hurt us, that is our witchly calling.

*   *   *

Sometimes, not often—maybe four or five times in a lifetime—you meet somebody who looks straight into you and through you. A gaze that renders you naked, stripped of opacity, of pretense, of guardedness; a gaze that locks you into a certain place and a certain time. Fucha Ñua was just such a person, and when the sky turns a certain shade of gray, I can feel his gaze still. Esteban and I had ridden through the heart of the isthmus between the lake and the ocean to reach a small homestead composed of a single small *ruka*. *Ruka* are the traditional Mapuche longhouses, thatched with reeds, with no windows or chimney, and with a single door facing the rising sun to the east. While most of my older friends had been born and raised in *ruka*, at the time I am describing and for at least the previous few decades, everybody had lived in wooden houses with corrugated zinc roofs. The most recent homes were *casas de subsidio*, "subsidized houses" provided by the Chilean state for the poorest rural families, most of whom in the south were Mapuche. You can still see many *ruka*, but they are now used as animal pens or outdoor kitchens; nobody would dream of living in them, or rather, nobody but Fucha Ñua. When we arrived, I was a little confused about where exactly he lived, but seeing no other buildings on the property, it became clear to me that this *ruka* was indeed where he stayed: a simple hearth on the dirt floor, a wooden bed in the far corner, no water, no electricity, just an old black kettle hanging from the rafters—rafters that were barely visible in the smoke-filled roof space.

Why we'd gone there, I can't remember. It may have been to tend to some animal, although I don't remember Fucha Ñua having any animals. Or it may have been to help him with some bureaucratic task, some form or other that needed filling out; but then again, Fucha Ñua had as little to do with the forces of bureaucracy as he could. Maybe Esteban just thought he'd be an interesting person for me to meet. He was a tall man, dressed in black. His clothes were old and worn, but he wore his poverty well; it seemed like an almost intentional act of self-presentation, both ascetic and aesthetic. He was old, maybe in his late sixties, maybe in his seventies, but he moved with an ease and a soft tread that belied his age. His skin was dark, and deeply lined, and only part of his face was visible under his battered black trilby. I seem to remember that he was missing an eye, or perhaps blind in one eye, but as I think back his face seems to always be just out of reach of my memory, always eclipsed by his gaze. Fucha Ñua means "Old Devil"; it was of course not his real name, but a nickname given to him by others, and here is why.

When he was a child, Fucha Ñua lived with his mother, a woman who was terribly feared by everybody for miles around. They all said that she was a witch, a *kalku*, driven by a lust for destruction and by spite. She was ostracized, and although people tolerated her small *ruka* on a worthless corner of land, they would avoid her at all costs. Fucha Ñua wouldn't believe the things that they said about her: the people she'd killed, the things she did at night, the things she became at night. But now, recounting this childhood again for my benefit (since Esteban and everybody else already knew the story well), he remembered things about her that, with the benefit of sixty or so years of hindsight, didn't seem right. She would make him do strange, incomprehensible things, to make him reveal to her the person he would one day become. She'd take him to the crossroads at dawn on St. John's Day, a feast that coincides with the Mapuche New Year, *We Tripantu*; the first person to appear coming along the road would be a kind of template for his future self. If it was a teacher, he'd become a teacher; if it was a thief, he too would take to robbing. His mother would watch for these premonitions anxiously and listen closely to his dreams, going quiet and digesting their possible meanings. But none of the answers she got ever seemed to truly satisfy her. So eventually she turned to *miyayatun*.

Miyayatun is a semi-occult ritual practice that people around the lake remember well but that nobody has carried out for decades. A young child, maybe six or seven years old, was given a tea of toasted *miyaya*, the hallucinogen known in English as jimson weed. After a while, the child would start hallucinating, or "become drunk," *molliñ*, as local people put it. And in the depth of its hallucination the child would act in certain ways, reaching for objects, reaching for people, reaching for words. These actions would be carefully interpreted in order to offer an accurate picture of the child's future path through life and their adult identity. Thus, a child who seized an empty wine carton from the floor would become a drunk; grabbing a hammer might imply a propensity for construction; picking up money was a sign of future wealth, and so on.

Fucha Ñua, so the story goes, did none of these things. Instead, once the *miyaya* had taken hold, he calmly reached into the fire that was burning on the floor in the center of the *ruka*, seized a flaming stick, and held it up to his mother, setting fire to her shawl. From that day forth, the woman was wary of her son, wary of what was to come. Fucha Ñua suffered. He suffered at the hands of his mother, and he suffered at the hands of those who said his mother was a witch. He was, they say, a good son, hardworking, and always ready to defend his mother's reputation despite the rumors that constantly circulated. Then one day, by now a teenager, returning early from work on somebody else's fields, he encountered something, his mother doing something, a thing that to this day is shrouded in silence, but that confirmed all of the rumors that he had spent his life up to that point denying. There was a struggle of one kind or other, a struggle that intensified and heated up until, in a rage, Fucha Ñua pushed his mother back into the *ruka*. She stumbled before falling headlong into the fire, burned by her son once more. Yet this time the vision of the *miyaya* was complete: she died of her injuries, and Fucha Ñua spent the next eleven years in jail for her murder.

He was now, many years later, a man alone, and it's hard to imagine him having ever been anything other than alone, so perfectly and aesthetically self-contained did he seem to be. Nevertheless, he had apparently married after leaving prison, a marriage that, although short-lived, produced a daughter. In fact, I happened to know both his ex-wife and his daughter: the ex-wife had eventually married a white Chilean who spoke no Mapudungun, while she spoke barely a word of Spanish; they say it was a happy marriage. And his daughter I remember hanging from my neck as we drunkenly danced in some place or other, a woman who seemed damaged in a way that I immediately sensed but realized I would never understand. She disappeared in Santiago a few years later, but will maybe one day reappear, as people lost to Santiago occasionally do. Fucha Ñua spoke to us outside; he looked at me under that gray Pacific sky, and I knew at once that he could see me for who I was, that he could see that my life was so inexorably different from his own, and I felt as if I was being beheld in the eyes of some predatory being, yet not in hunger or rage but rather pity. And who, I wondered, affronted, was he to pity me? I'd assumed I was the one to gaze, not be gazed upon, and the reversal of direction startled me. Maybe he had seen things for what they really were, moving from vision to truth to self and its absence.

*　*　*

The land here is perforated with morality. Some places are "good," some places are "bad." What exactly this means, I've never entirely understood, for when people refer to places in such a way, they're speaking in a register that gestures to something beyond what can be put precisely into words, to an embodied feeling as much as an idea, neither to a memory nor an event but to peaks and troughs in the topography of a moral plain. There was a gate between the top field and the long field that stretched toward the school, which was one such "bad" place. The gate was situated in a dense thicket of *folo* trees, dark trees with such dense foliage that light was forced to slip in under the sides of the thicket rather than penetrating from above. The roots of these trees had become entangled with one another, held each other in rough embraces, and now seemed to form tortured and writhing animal shapes. The path on either side of the gate would

become so churned up into viscous mud over the course of the winter that anybody on foot was forced to find their way through the
dense thicket that lay next to it. The darkness here in the midst of the
thicket was intensified by the brightness of the open fields that lay on
both sides of it, broad fields on high ground providing vistas as far
away as the distant volcanoes of the Cordillera.

It was quiet and sheltered in the thicket, but not in a way that
made one feel welcome. It felt undeniably strange, and even the animals quickened their pace when being driven through it. Birdsong
seemed absent or muted. I wasn't surprised when Marta told me that
there was "evil" there; it seemed to resonate with the way this small
stand of trees on either side of a gate made both people and animals
feel. Neither Marta nor anybody else ever specified what kind of "evil"
we were talking about, or whether this evil simply inhabited the place
or the place itself was evil. These kinds of clarifications would have
been beside the point: a futile attempt to tie a vaporous ambiguity
down to an identity that, almost by definition, it couldn't have. The
word *weküfe* is used to refer to what we might call demons or evil
spirits, and in some specific instances, to the Devil himself. But these
identities bleed into one another; a story that started off being about
several *weküfe* would, over the course of its telling, morph into a
story about a single demon, or even just a place. What was important
was not the precise nature of the being—there could be no definitive
taxonomy of evil—but the simple fact that it should be avoided or
placated and that one should not dally when passing nearby.

I was more than happy to keep to this injunction and always
increased my pace when walking through. However, when on horseback, one was often forced to dismount to remove the top pole of the
gate, lead the horse through, and then replace the pole. This always
made me nervous; it seemed like the optimum moment for evil to
strike. As soon as I was back in the saddle, I would spur the horse
into a gallop to put as much ground between myself and the gate as
possible. People had seen things there: some said that they'd seen a

huaso, the Spanish term for the traditional Chilean cowboy, a euphemistic reference to what is known in Mapudungun as a *witranalwe*, a raised spirit. Such creatures have a material presence, painstakingly crafted by witches from human femurs scavenged from cemeteries. They are then sold by these witches to landowners, serving their new masters by guarding their flocks and allowing them to multiply and make their owners rich. During the day, the *witranalwe* can shrink to occupy a small jar or a leather pouch, and only extends to its full human height at nighttime, when taking up its work once more. There is, as there always is, a catch to employing the services of such a creature: their taste for blood is insatiable. They eventually turn on the flocks that they are supposed to protect and, when that source of blood has been exhausted, they turn upon their owner himself, if not his family. Once the owner has been brought to ruin, the *witranalwe* returns to the witch who gave it life.

Others had mentioned rumors of an *antümalen*, another malevolent being moving through worlds of half-spoken understandings, glimpses, and night. I was less concerned with the *antümalen* for the simple reason that it was understood to be a creature of light, *antümalen* meaning "girl of the sun." Yet despite the assertion of this connection to the sun, she was always described as "shining like the moon," *küyen reke*, a false sun born of darkness. People said that if you were walking along and happened to see a bright, white pebble, maybe a piece of quartz, you should never pick it up or even touch it. To do so would be to bring it to life as an *antümalen*, a shining young girl bringing death in her wake.

The catalogue of malevolent beings occupying the Mapuche world could never be exhausted. They slipped and morphed into one another, each one taking on characteristics that seemed to resonate with certain anxieties woven into the social fabric. Thus *witranalwe*, dressed as they were in the garb of the Chilean cowboy, spoke of colonialism, the usurpation of land, and the hidden costs of an increasingly unequal distribution of wealth in the rural south. Likewise, the *antümalen* cast both literal and figurative light on the strange plight of young women, often faced with a choice between unhappy marriages far from their natal communities or migration to low-paid menial work in the big cities. But these quasi-Marxist explanations for the supernatural could only ever be partial; there was always an excess that could not be accounted for. People were more than capable of coming up with their own critiques of these social issues, and the structural problems constraining Mapuche life were a mystery to no one. Yet these beings persisted, corralled by witches, occupying that space beyond the rational, beyond language, gestured toward and feared. And just the slightest touch of the softest twilight breeze, gently passing over me as I replaced the top pole of the gate, would raise the hairs on the back of my neck. Of what I was afraid, I was never quite sure, and that perhaps was the reason to fear it.

*   *   *

Mapuche society has undergone many profound changes over the past few decades. More than half a million Mapuche people now live in the Chilean capital, Santiago, and many others are spread across other towns and cities throughout southern Chile and western Argentina. This hemorrhaging of the rural population has its roots in the acute land shortage resulting from decades of state-sponsored theft and usurpation by ranching and logging interests. Young people these days frequently have little choice but to leave for work in the cities, orchards, and vineyards of the north. This dramatic shift in Mapuche society has led to great anxiety about cultural loss: fewer and fewer people are speaking the Mapuche language, fewer and fewer people participate in the rural economy, and many young people in the cities, battered by a persistent and ubiquitous racism, start to describe themselves not as Mapuche but simply as *sureños,* "southerners." Yet despite these turbulent upheavals and specters of loss, two constants from the rural south remain among these generations of urban migrants: a concern with witchcraft, and a concern with dreams—for the two are bound together: it is in the space of dreaming that the witch emerges.

One of the first phrases I ever learned in Mapudungun was *Chem pewmaymi?* "What did you dream?" This would always be the first question that Marta asked of me when we sat down for breakfast. If we could each bring up memories of whatever dreams we'd had the night before, we would share them and collectively try to piece together their meaning, what they foretold, what advice might be extracted from them. Dreams, *pewma*, are understood to be the wanderings of an aspect of the self—sometimes called *alwe*, sometimes called *am*—not just through time and space but through different registers of being. In dreams, we might see things as they really are; animals or plants revealed as people, objects as living, the living as dead. Dreams allow us to seep into other ways of seeing the world, or perhaps to seep into other worlds.

But dreams can also function in a premonitory capacity, and these were the dreams that seemed to come to me. One night, I dreamt that I was with my father, a man I had neither seen nor barely thought about for several years previously. In the dream, he wasn't speaking, and his hair was whiter than I remembered. He was sitting propped up against the *folo* tree next to the lake by which I would often sit and rest. I was with him, but not really engaged in any way; we neither spoke to each other nor looked at each other. I seemed to be slightly elevated, looking down upon him from the level of the tree's highest branches. Radiating from the trunk of the tree were long ropes, and at the end of each rope was tied a horse. The horses were of different colors: some gray, some bay, some chestnut, and some white, yet for some reason I was particularly struck by the fact that none were black. As I watched, the horses started to move in a counterclockwise direction around the tree. They gradually accelerated until they were at a flat-out gallop. The ropes wrapped around my father, and as the horses galloped, the ropes tightened further and further. I was now having to hop over the ropes, like a child in a long-forgotten playground game. When I looked back at my father, he had been completely covered by the ropes and I could no longer see him.

My usual experience of being asked each morning about my dreams was one of disappointment at myself for being unable to remember anything. Occasionally, I would have a few fragmentary images or feelings, but rarely did they constitute a clear narrative. I was relieved to finally have something to say, yet at the same time something about the dream would not leave me, an unease or disquiet that I couldn't quite put my finger on. "You should phone him straightaway," was Juan's advice, upon listening to my dream while intently sucking his *mate* tea through a metal straw. "He's probably dead," Marta chimed in bluntly. I realized then that it wasn't the possibility of his death that alarmed me; if he were dead, I would at least have a tidy future anecdote about the premonitory potential of dreams. There was something else. I should probably have gone up to the school and tried to get through on the pay phone, but I didn't. I didn't have his number, although I'm sure I could have gotten it with a couple of quick calls if I'd really tried. It was later confirmed to me that my father, who was in his eighties, had suffered the onset of dementia following heart surgery. He had slowly become locked into himself, withdrawing into a past world, a world of memory. He sat in a chair and did not move, staring emptily at the television even when it was turned off. The dream was not exactly a premonition of this, for I was already more or less aware that he was in this situation—it was rather a rephrasing of it, a bringing into the foreground something about my relationship to him that I understood emotionally but struggled to put into words. Marta was making *sopaipillas* that morning, round disks of dough fried in fat, or *yiwiñ kofke*, "fat bread" in Mapudungun. Something in my expression prompted her to give me an extra fried egg to accompany the hot, crisp bread, full of steam that escaped when you broke it.

Dreams are the traces not only of the outer wanderings of an inner soul but of the intrusion of other souls into one's inner being. It is through dreams that *ngen*—the guardian spirits that personify places, plants, and animals—reveal themselves in human form and communicate with the dreamer. Juan told me that a few years previously, a *triwke*, a small hawk, had been perched on the tall pines at the back of the patio and would swoop leisurely down to pick off Marta's newly hatched chicks. Juan took out his old shotgun and shot the bird, not killing it but clipping its wing, so that it flew away with a strange, looping flight. That night, Juan dreamt, and in his dream a young man came to him with an exasperated look on his face and annoyance in his voice. "Look what you've done to me," said the young man, looking down at his broken and bloodied arm. "Surely a hungry person has the right to eat?" This was the *ngen* of the hawk reprimanding Juan, who has never shot another hawk since.

The *ngen* of the area between the lake and the ocean is personified by a great black bull, *kuru toru*, and when it is time to hold the fertility ritual, the bull is said to enter people's dreams. Its bellowing reverberates throughout the night, both within sleep and outside it, permeating the soft membranes between this world and its parallel others. These are the dreams that people must act on: to ignore them or resist them makes one sick, an illness without clear cause and without clear symptoms but potentially fatal nonetheless. The black bull demands; it reminds its people of who they are, of where they belong, of what they are a part of. A friend with a role in the ritual once told me that the bull pursued him through his dreams to the extent that all he had to do was close his eyes, and even while awake, he could feel the vibrations of the bull's stamping and bellowing in his guts.

Yet the appearance of *ngen* in dreams can also be a sign of welcome. My friend Juana told me that decades before, when she had first married and moved to her husband's community, she had suffered from great anxiety. What if the place did not welcome her?

What if her new husband and in-laws beat her? What if nothing grew? In the first week of her marriage, she had a dream. She dreamt that a young woman invited her into a *ruka* longhouse, and laid out upon a table inside the house was a great stack of produce: carrots, garlic, chilies, celery, spinach; there were even bunches of flowers. The table overflowed with providence. The young woman smiled and beckoned Juana toward her. Juana understood then that the young woman was the *ngen* of her new home, a home tucked into the woods by the shore of the lake. And that the *ngen* would provide for her, would be sure to bestow abundance upon her and let her garden fill with all kinds of produce. And so it has been; Juana has made a home for herself, raised her children and grandchildren, and her garden has always been productive and bountiful. All of these years later, Juana remembers that dream with a smile of love and gratitude to the place that she now recognizes as home.

Dreams can make us stronger, can provide us with necessary wisdom if we are open. But this openness makes us vulnerable, and it is into this space that the witch enters. Whenever I had to pass through Santiago, I would stay with a Mapuche friend, Javiera, in an old, converted garage at the side of someone's house in the poorest part of the capital. She had fled north to the city after her marriage had disintegrated, her husband found beaten and left for dead in a field, damaged and losing his mind. Here in the city she worked and worked and was abused in all the ways poor migrants to cities are abused. She told people she wasn't Mapuche anymore, just a southerner, that she couldn't understand a word of the language in which she'd been raised. But her dreams were always of the south, of what used to be home. And here in her dreams, the witch would pursue her. What everybody agreed on was that a witch had stolen her ex-husband's mind. His family blamed her family, while her family blamed them back. She did not know; she could not see the witch. In her dreams there was always a figure just out of sight, a glimpse of something dark before the contours and context of the dream shifted. She wasn't sure if this was something sent by the witch or if it was the witch itself, biding its time but always there waiting and watching, poised to destroy.

*   *   *

I was tired, and with the steady rhythm of the horse's gait I drew myself inward, pulling my jacket close around my shoulders, letting my eyelids droop. The crunch of hooves on gravel filled my ears like a slow scrape of waves, blending into the distant background of the waves of the ocean, a few miles to the west. The horse knew her way home, so I let the reins hang loosely, cupping them in my hand, feeling the soft tug back and forth as her head and shoulders accompanied each stride. The southern constellations shone above as we—my mare Quintrala and I—moved slowly and calmly along the road through the island. The homesteads we passed were in darkness, standing out as silhouettes against the greater dark of the night. Night here was always darkest near its earthly margins, the sky lightening as one's gaze moved up toward the great *wenu lewfu*, the heavenly river, a great swath of sparkling stars opening the heavens like a wound of light. At ground level, however, it was all shapes and shadows; trees and houses would suddenly move, revealing themselves as cattle or horses, heads resting on wire fences, staring out at the road.

After a couple of miles of this soporific motion, I reached the sharp left-hand turn for the steep slope that led down to the fording point across the lake, to get back to the isthmus and home. One side of the path was marked by a thick eucalyptus plantation owned by a retired schoolteacher, a plantation that seemed to grow exponentially year by year. On the other side was a small abandoned homestead that had belonged to a man named Nalka whom I had known in my earlier days at the lake. Nalka had died the previous year, dropping stone dead, drink in hand, at a football tournament. His friends had stood around, open-mouthed, wondering how what had been could be so suddenly gone, Nalka facedown in the mud. He had neither wife nor children, and although his land had been plowed and sown by a cousin, his house was slowly going back to the earth.

The steep path down to the ford was composed of mud and gravel, truckload after truckload of gravel being spread by the municipality in the winter months, but rain and gravity combining to wash it all down to the lake within weeks. The central portion of the path had become nothing more than a muddy slide, useless to all. Either on foot or on horseback, people clung to the ruts on either side created by the occasional 4x4 trucks that braved the crossing in all but the wettest months. On horseback, one simply had to trust the horse, but even then, its stumbles and slips would jolt the rider to alertness. The awareness that this challenge was to come had already started to rouse me as we turned onto the start of the path to begin our descent, the tall trees making it almost pitch black. A sudden shift in the air to the right of my head made me contract in an instant, like a drop of oil in water, pulling the reins tight, lifting my feet in the heavy wooden stirrups. Again, something cut the air around my head, the mare tautening with an explosive tension. And again, what sounded like a rapid cross-cutting of blades in circles around us, and we were off.

There was no need to touch my spurs to her flank; she simply bolted and I let her. Headlong down the slope, through the darkness, slipping and skidding, stumbling and sliding. I locked my legs around her belly, let the reins loose. We hit the water hard, her broad chest making a bow wave, spray soaking me as I pulled back on the reins, turning her slowly into a halt. We were out of the trees, at the bottom of the slope, and standing in the middle of the submerged path across this part of the lake, to either side of us thick beds of rushes reflecting the creamy light of the night sky. I could see the lights of Juan and Marta's homestead still blazing across the lake in front of me, while the dark eucalyptus-filled mass of the island stood behind. Before I could gather my thoughts, or feel the creeping cold of my soaked clothes, the disturbance in the air returned, a whirring noise, a breath against my cheek, a drone, a wail. I looked in every direction but could see nothing: no bird, no bat. I dug my spurs into the mare's flank, but again, she needed no encouragement as we took off again. The great effort of galloping through the chest-high water exaggerated the motion as she lurched backward and forward, sending waves crashing through the reedbeds on either side.

As we reached the far side, her movements eased and our speed increased as the brackish water poured off us. The lights of the homestead flickered to the south, but several barbed wire fences along the way forced a lengthy detour, on horseback at least, up the steep path to the school and then back down. Like its counterpart on the island side, this steep path was little more than a washed-out mudslide, the scene of several fatal accidents over the years. The trees surrounding this path were not the tall, thin eucalyptus of before but the dense, thick foliage of native trees—*folo, triwe, koyam*—reaching toward each other across the space above the muddy ascent. Again, I brought the horse to a halt, but once more the whirring air surrounded us. Panic grew inside me, augmenting the adrenaline created by the gallop through the lake. A possibility nagged at me, a possibility of something once overheard, laughed about, then dismissed.

Somebody, somewhere, had told me of a woman who could not sleep. She drifted in and out, hovering beyond rest, her head filling with strange dreams, strange sensations. She grew more and more tired, and her husband more and more distant. Her desires—for food, for sex, for life itself—all faded away and all she desired was sleep. Anxious relatives took her soiled clothes to a shaman in the city, yet he provided neither diagnosis nor cure; he simply told them to observe her husband. They took every opportunity to watch him; they watched him work, they watched him eat, they watched him drink, but he was the same somewhat distant man as always. Finally, the relatives told the woman of their concerns, of what the shaman had said, and persuaded her to watch her husband at night. That evening she drank *mate* after *mate*, hoping the bitter stimulant would keep her alert. Yet

once in bed, the strange non-sleep overcame her. In the middle of the
night, a soft breeze from an open window woke her, and as she turned
on her side the cause of her problem was revealed: the body of her
husband, gently rising and falling with each breath, but missing its
head. He was, it transpired, a *chon-chon*, a form of witch whose head
was able to sprout wings and depart from its body at night while the
rest of the earth lay sleeping. In this form the *chon-chon* could spy
and wreak damage upon its victims, either for some kind of personal
gain or just through pure spite. *Chon-chon* share their name with barn
owls, which likewise appear in the southern night as ghostly heads
with wings. The woman then closed the window firmly and awaited
the frustrated tapping of her husband's head at the window before
dawn, stranded from its body. How the story ends, I've forgotten, or
perhaps I was never told, but I had actually met this sleepless woman,
now a quiet old lady with no husband.

As we galloped up the steep slope, my sense that this invisible
beating fluttering by my head was the *chon-chon* only grew. When
we slowed, it slowed; when we speeded up, it matched us. By the
time we reached the top of the slope by the gates of the school, I was
desperate. As I turned the horse back at the hairpin bend toward the
homestead, I was relieved to see the gate open; the thought of having
to dismount was too much to bear. I put in one last flat-out gallop,
scared now not only of the *chon-chon* but of the poor mare's heart
bursting. Rounding the hill to the front of the house, I slowed, but I
knew even before I felt the whirring of its wings around my face that
we had not and could not outrun it. I threw the reins over the nearest fencepost, slipping in the mud as I dismounted, and burst into
the kitchen and the smell of fried bread. Marta absorbed the sight
of me, listened to my babbling account, and then, with a calm she
had never before displayed, disappeared to my room. She returned
with my shotgun and a fistful of cartridges, walked past me to the
still-open door, and fired each cartridge, one by one, into the night
sky, the dark trees, the stars. She did not take aim, but turned her

face away with each pull of the trigger. For it is said to be sound, not pellets nor bullets, that drives evil away. After all, who can shoot what is never really fully there? It was this thunder, a thunder that reverberated off our tin roof and wooden walls, that forced the *chon-chon* away—the same thunder that provides the Mapuche word for shotgun, *tralka*. Juan walked into breakfast the next morning not having heard a thing.

* * *

I do like a good party. The fact that Juan and Marta's eldest son, Mateo, shares a birthday with me—we are exactly ten years apart—seemed like an opportunity too good to miss. We would hold our party jointly: he would invite his friends and I would invite mine, although there was such an overlap between these two categories that the distinction seemed redundant. As Mateo didn't have any money, I would pay for the party. This involved buying drinks and a large pig. Once people know that you're in the market for a pig, prices rise sharply. In the end, however, Juan and I managed to purchase a large red-haired pig from an old woman somewhere in the center of the isthmus, an area so criss-crossed by almost identical paths that I would always lose myself there, imagining the ocean to be in the direction of the mountains. The pig was reluctant to come with us, and we ended up with me pulling it by a rope while Juan swatted furiously at its broad russet backside, as we progressed slowly homeward. In addition to the pig, I'd asked Marta to buy drinks on her latest excursion into the port. Mateo didn't seem very impressed with the size of the pig, but as I was paying, he opted to remain silent.

In the weeks preceding the party, I'd made various journeys across all the communities on the western side of the lake to invite friends. People would not respond to paper invitations, nor would they accept a secondhand invitation; only a direct, face-to-face invitation from the host of the party would do. I invited everybody I knew, everybody I could think of, everyone I'd met. Working from the assumption that only about half the people invited ever turn up, I felt that the numbers would somehow regulate themselves, that there was some self-limiting, thermostatic mechanism inherent somewhere in this whole process. But above all, I was mortified at the possibility of offending people, of failing to invite somebody whom I should have. People didn't exactly give me a response as such, more a kind of acknowledgment that the event would indeed take place, but without any clear commitment as to whether they'd be there or not. While my worries were that nobody would come, Marta's were that everybody would come and, thus, that we'd run out of food. This would of course reflect on her. "That pig is so skinny," she complained. "I thought you'd bought a *huacho*; that's just a bag of bones!" A *huacho* is a pig that's been enclosed in a pen and fed several times a day until it reaches truly monstrous proportions. Just under its skin, a thick layer of deep, rich fat develops that can then be rendered down for cooking purposes. My pig was unfortunately no *huacho*. I didn't think it looked quite as malnourished as Marta claimed, but I was beginning to wonder about what we'd do if everybody I'd invited did indeed turn up. I was starting to appreciate the fact that Mateo didn't have many friends, but when I was foolish enough to mention this to him, he pointed out that he actually had lots of friends and that he'd invited even more people than I had. Who these people were or how he knew them, I had no idea, but it meant that Juan and I were obliged to set out once more, this time to buy a back-up pig. The pig we ended up coming home with was if anything skinnier and scrawnier than the one we'd bought the previous day. Nevertheless, it was something.

The next day was my birthday; I imagine I was maybe 25 or 26 by this time. Maybe even 27. It was a beautiful summer's morning, something only the southern hemisphere can confer upon those of us with December birthdays. The sky was such a deep blue that if you stared at it for too long you felt as if you'd tip forward and fall into it.

The sun was now peeking over the skyline of the island to the east, and a thin fog was gently steaming itself into oblivion from the surface of the lake. It was time to kill the pigs, or at least one of them. I had persuaded myself that it should be me who killed the pig, partly because I felt it made clear my custodianship of the party, but also, it has to be said, because I was intrigued to find out whether or not I'd be able to do it. When I was younger, I would frequently faint at the sight of blood, my own or anybody else's. I was deeply concerned about this and felt that it made me, in so many ways, less of a person; or rather, it confirmed me as exactly the kind of person I feared I might be. I wanted to act upon the world, not be acted upon. Perhaps this idea had its roots in a kind of masculinity that has long since passed from favor, or perhaps its roots lie elsewhere; I don't know. Whatever its source, I was under the impression that real men kill things, they engage in the world through its destruction, and this seemed to me to be an opportunity to prove to myself that I, too, could destroy.

Killing a pig cleanly isn't quite as easy as you might imagine. First of all, you have to catch it. Marta threw some oats out onto the patio and a crowd of pigs and chickens soon came running. The red of the pigs blended into the red of the earth and in the chaos and confusion it wasn't entirely clear which pig it was we were trying to catch. I managed to snag the nearest one to me, only to have Mateo scream at me from the doorway that that was his pig and we couldn't kill it. "But it's your birthday too," I shouted. "Yes, but you're rich," he replied. I let the pig go. Eventually Juan managed to grab the correct pig by its mud-covered hind leg. It thrashed around like a fish on a line, screaming its high-pitched squeal, and who could blame it? Juan quickly bound its four feet together, tied another piece of twine around its snout, and together we lifted it onto a small wooden bench. It lay on its side, snorting through its tightly bound mouth. The goal was to stab the pig in the chest and pierce its heart; it would then die quickly and blood would pour out of its body, leaving the meat "clean." Several times in the past, I'd seen people stab the chest, but miss the heart. This wasn't good for anybody, least of all the pig.

The pig on the bench fixed me with its eye, a beautiful hazel eye. It struck me then just how like human eyes are the eyes of pigs. Juan once told me a story: that many years ago the Virgin Mary descended to earth to see how everybody was getting along. She went from community to community until she arrived at one particular place where, although it was midday, everybody was still in bed asleep. Such was her anger at their laziness that she turned them all into pigs, and that's why, to this very day, pigs have human eyes. Juan's half-brother Babyface had turned up from somewhere; people, myself included, were often drawn to the sound of pigs' screaming just as wasps are drawn to cider: there is the prospect of something good. He gave me a large glass of what I imagine was pisco mixed with Coca-Cola. I took a long gulp, returned the glass, and then plunged the knife into the pig and up toward where I imagined its heart to be. A warm stripe of blood arced out of its chest and laid itself neatly along my forearm, in perfect alignment. I twisted the knife, and another stripe surged out, this time covering my boots. The dogs crowded around, trying to lick the hot, steaming blood from my arms, my boots, the compacted earth of the patio floor. I pushed the knife to one side to allow the blood to continue flowing from the hole in the pig's heart, deep inside. Its struggles declined and it ceased moving altogether, until its body suddenly tensed in one final, shuddering spasm.

I stood back while Juan poured a kettle of boiling water over the dead pig to soften its hard bristles and allow them to be torn out by hand. He and Babyface worked quickly from head to toe, short neat tugs setting free clumps of red hair. Marta filled the kettle again from a large pot on the stove and the final patches of hair around the trotters were removed. Juan gently took the knife from my hand, rinsed it, and set to work removing each trotter with a quick slash either side of the joint. He then cut off the head and passed it to one of Babyface's children, who proceeded to balance it on top of their own head and dance about like a clown. A neat cut was made on the pig from throat to genitals, and the bluish entrails spilled out into a waiting bucket. Juan's youngest son, Camilo, was instructed to go and dump them as far away from the house as possible, which turned out not to be very far away at all, as the cacophony of barking from every dog in the surrounding area burst out from behind the line of pine trees only fifty yards away. Finally, the pig was further divided up and taken into the kitchen. I looked at my hands; the blood had flowed into every line and crack, seeming to spell out my own life across my palms and into my nails.

To host a party successfully, one needs to be a master of pace and timing. Resources must flow, but not too quickly. People should have to wait, but never too long. I had several large plastic five-liter bottles of red wine in my room, which I could decant into glass bottles or else mix with Coke in jugs to produce *sangre de jote*, "vulture's blood." I'd also bought a couple of special bottles of wine, wine packaged in neither cardboard nor plastic but the luxury and expense of glass. These were for special guests, people whom I really wanted to either thank, flatter, or impress.

The topic of alcohol is a sensitive one for many Mapuche people, who are acutely aware of the racist stereotypes, held by white Chileans, of the Mapuche as drunken and lazy. In fact, alcohol consumption is no higher in Mapuche communities than it is among non-Indigenous communities elsewhere in rural Chile. And indeed, many Mapuche communities are now completely teetotal, with alcohol strictly prohibited from ritual events. However, at that time, twenty-five years ago, alcohol was an undeniable part of my life at the lake. While its negative effects on myself and others will be apparent in the pages to come, it would be disingenuous to overlook its positive effects: not only the role played by the exchanging of wine in creating and maintaining friendships, but also the simple joy of having a drink with people you love. In this vein, I was thinking that perhaps some guests would bring wine as well, but the first people to arrive—Luis and Juana—presented me with a carrier bag full of string beans and a half dozen eggs. Their son, Gaspar, better known as *Ngürü* (Fox), was with them, but quickly disappeared into Mateo's room to admire the Colo-Colo football shirt that had been my birthday gift to him.

More and more people started to arrive, and to each new arrival I gave a glass and a bottle filled from my supply. Some people brought me the odd carton of wine; most brought me nothing but good wishes. Marta was busy handing out plates of food to Juan, who in turn handed them out to guests. This should have been my duty but I was sorely neglecting it, finding it difficult to get away from sharing the wine I'd been given while at the same time handing out wine to new arrivals. It got darker and I, along with everybody around me, got drunker. I remember sitting outside singing an *ül* I'd heard—a genre of autobiographical song—in the company of Juan's step-mother. Rather embarrassingly, it turned out that unbeknownst to me, what I was singing was actually *her* song, telling the story of *her* life, but rather than be offended, thankfully she seemed quite flattered that anybody else would choose to sing her song.

I remembered the bottles of nice wine I'd put aside to give to especially honored guests. One was for Esteban, with whom I'd first lodged at the lake, and the other was for my friend Sebastián. I'd presented Sebastián with his bottle earlier in the evening, and he'd drunk it on the spot. Yet now I found him berating me for inviting him over from the island but not giving him anything. "But don't you remember?" I said, "I gave you a bottle of expensive wine when you got here, not even an hour ago?" "You didn't give me anything, you people are all the same," he gruffly asserted. I wasn't entirely sure who "you people" referred to: people from the isthmus? white people? "Just ignore him, he's drunk," his wife contributed. But being somewhat drunk myself, I wouldn't let it go. I rescued the empty bottle from outside and confronted him with it. "Here, this is what I gave you!" I shouted. Despite being confronted with the evidence, he continued to grumble, and I continued to feel myself the victim of a great and terrible injustice.

Going outside into the night to calm down, I met Mateo and a couple of his friends at the entrance to the patio. They were smoking cigarettes, *petrem* in Mapudungun, a vice relatively rare among people in this area. I took a drag and exhaled into the depth of the southern summer night. It was at this point that all hell broke loose. A neighbor, Pedro, had come out of the house to relieve himself and, seeing his son smoking, slapped the cigarette from his hand and then slapped his face. Chaos ensued: father and son grabbed each other in a vicious headlock, both refusing to yield and shouting vociferously at each other. The dogs crowded around barking, absorbing the excitement, but not sure which master to follow. And the noise of the dogs brought a drunken crowd out from the house onto the patio to witness what Marta would later refer to as "the disgrace," as if it could somehow be linguistically cordoned off in time, placed in some kind of temporal quarantine. I found myself wedged between the son and Pedro in their ferocious embrace, trying hopelessly to pull them apart. The calm I feel in this kind of situation always strikes me as completely incongruous with how I view myself, but it's a calm rooted in resignation rather than resilience. Eventually Mateo joined in, and together we pulled the errant son to the ground, while Pedro stumbled away. Mateo had ended up on top of me, and there we lay, the two birthday boys in a drunken heap in the mud. Before we could stop her, Marta's mother, Constanza, dumped a bucketful of cold water over Mateo and me, soaking us both in the process. The crowd ebbed back into the house, but for me the party was over. For Mateo, too, the fun had ended and he ran crying into the woods.

*   *   *

The perverse desire to dominate through destruction that I'd first felt about killing the pig now seemed to shift form, as I soon became obsessed with hunting or, rather, with the idea of hunting. I asked a friend in America to send me some old hunting outfitters' catalogues, and I would stay up late at night imagining myself fully equipped with equipment crafted from the finest bridle leather, striding across some range in the Rocky Mountains with a faithful hunting dog, retiring only to sip the best bourbon by an open fire. The world around me divided itself into things I could shoot and those I could not. Of course, before this fantasy could congeal into reality, I needed to get myself a gun. There were two obstacles in my way: first, I was a foreigner and thus anticipated even more complex bureaucracy than usual to get a gun permit, and second, I lived in an area where hunting was at least theoretically banned.

The task of getting a gun permit involved a trip to some kind of military headquarters in the regional capital, Temuco. I was expecting the usual interminable bureaucratic wait, but I was ushered into a small office straightaway. A surprisingly friendly soldier pointed out to me that Chileans would have their criminal records checked before a permit was issued, but as I was a foreigner they had no way of checking such records and would therefore just give me the benefit of the doubt. "You're not a murderer, are you?" he asked, somewhat jokingly (or at least I hoped he was joking). I suspected that even back then, before the so-called "Mapuche conflict" had escalated, he would not have given this same friendliness or benefit of the doubt to any of my Mapuche friends back at the lake. (Just recently, in 2018, Esteban, by now well into his seventies, had his small rural homestead stormed by an elite squad of heavily armed riot police and was prosecuted simply for possessing an antique 1930s shotgun that he'd inherited from his father.) The issue of living within an area where hunting was banned didn't seem to be a problem either. In fact, neither this soldier nor anybody I knew back at the lake turned out to be aware of this prohibition at all.

With permit in hand, I then made my way to a long-established agricultural outfitter a few blocks away. Generations of Mapuche people from throughout the region had stared through the windows of this very store, fantasizing over the seemingly infinite selection of all the necessary goods for rural life: saddles, bridles, and reins; plow-shares, hoes, and spreaders; antibiotics, vaccines, and vitamin sup-plements; cartridges, knives, and guns. I myself had frequently gazed longingly at their displays while passing the hours waiting for the bus back to the port, especially the guns with their ornate silver fixings and walnut stocks. This was as close as I could get to accessing the hunts-man's life I felt destined to live. Unfortunately, these luxurious, hand-crafted, double-barreled European models were beyond my budget, so I purchased instead a mass-produced, single-barreled, 16-gauge shot-gun made in Brazil. It was cheap, but it was beautiful to me.

I also purchased a gun bag and a box of cartridges, but even hidden in its bag, the gun still looked unmistakably like a gun. So I wrapped it in a couple of the ubiquitous pink-orange potato sacks for the bus ride back to the port. Mateo was waiting for me when I got off the bus by the school. Most teenage boys like playing with guns, and Mateo was no exception. I insisted on waiting at least until we got home to take the gun out of its bag, but no sooner had we done so than Mateo insisted on tearing into the box of cartridges. We set up an empty beer bottle on an old tree stump at the far side of the patio. A sudden nervousness had gripped me, so I didn't object when Mateo insisted on taking the first shot. I had underestimated the noise that a shotgun makes. An explosive boom filled the air and ricocheted back to us from across the other side of the gully. A sec-ond later, the same sound returned to us from the island beyond the reedbeds of the lake. These deep, echoing booms were accompanied by the delicate tinkling of a thousand shards of brown glass, cascad-ing onto the hard patio all around us, as the beer bottle evaporated into thin air.

Marta was the first to come running. "My bottles! My bottles! You're shooting my bottles!" she screamed. "I haven't got enough for the full crate of empties now!" We'd overlooked the fact that Marta had to return every glass bottle to avoid having to repay the deposit now lost in the glass splinters at her feet. Juan was next. "This place is covered in glass! The animals are going to shred their feet!" Mateo trudged forlornly back up to the house to get a broom with which to at least minimize the hazard. When he got back I helped him, collecting as much of the glass-filled dust as we could in bits of rolled-up cardboard and taking it to the rubbish pit behind the house. Despite his parents' anger, he was still buzzing from the thrill of the shooting, a grin spread wide across his face.

The power to destroy, it turned out, was an addiction. So later that day, once the coolness of evening had spread itself out upon the hill, I wandered down to the *mallíñ*, the swampy pond where ducks would sometimes feed. It was not ducks that I was after, though, but the small California quail that clustered there together in groups of ten or so. In the past, groups of these small birds had often run across the path away from the homestead, across the stubble, and down toward the pond. I figured that even an inexperienced hunter like myself was bound to hit one of them, so closely bunched were their black-and-white bodies, their drooping crests. These California quail, as their name suggests, are not native to Chile but were introduced to a small ranch near Valparaiso in the late nineteenth century by a Dutch rancher. They escaped, and spread rapidly southward toward Patagonia and eastward over the Cordillera into Argentina, filling the Southern Cone with their pied commotion.

The red earth of the track was further reddened by the late summer light, and against this redness there burst a sudden profusion of black and white as a small gang of quail raced across the pathway in front of me. I instinctively raised the shotgun and fired into the midst of them, kicking up a cloud of red dust. Once the dust had subsided, I advanced, wondering how many I'd hit: maybe three, perhaps four? Yet there was nothing but a strange scuff mark across the ground, not a quail nor even a feather to be seen. I was deeply puzzled; what bothered me wasn't just that I'd missed, but the fact that I couldn't quite understand *how* I'd missed. That evening, I dug out a guide to wing shooting that my friend had kindly included with the old catalogues. Apparently, the act of aiming is a red herring when it comes to shotguns; the entire process is based on our instinctive ability to point at something, thus successful shooting comes from thinking of the shotgun as simply an extension of your arm, or even finger. You shouldn't take aim along the gun's sights but simply point and shoot from the shoulder in one seamless, swinging motion, following the target and then edging just in front of it before squeezing the trigger.

The following evening, I went out again. I was hoping to catch some rabbits, because the oncoming dusk seemed to be the time at which they were most active. The steep slope down from the big wheat field toward the ford seemed to be full of rabbit holes, so that was the direction in which I headed, keeping low to avoid my silhouette casting a long shadow in the rapidly fading light. At this time of day, the colors and details of the vegetation along the lake's edge started to blur together, so that individual plants became indistinguishable and the scene formed a gray-green backdrop. The temperature had dropped quite quickly and I was wishing that I'd brought a jacket. Some rabbits moved at the far end of the slope, their burrows near a fallen cypress tree that for some reason or other had been left to rot rather than sawn into planks. I was sorely tempted to take a shot, but they were just a little too far away, and as I moved closer they caught sight or scent of me and hopped away.

As I retraced my steps back up the slope, a gray movement caught my attention below. I stared hard, back toward the lake, but could see nothing until it moved again, a hare. It sensed my presence and bolted along the line of the lakeshore in front of me. Placing my faith now in the power of instinct, I swung the shotgun up and along, accelerated to just in front of the hare's path, and pulled the trigger. The shot boomed across the lake and echoed back as a thousand birds took flight. The hare cartwheeled a few yards, and then stopped, dead. I wasn't quite sure what to feel; a sense of accomplishment, achievement, and possibility, sure; but also guilt and shock at the violence of this act of sheer destruction. The hare's huge black-and-amber eyes were open, but staring blankly, the spark of life lost. It was a hefty animal, far bigger than the rabbits that I'd originally targeted. I picked it up by its lean hind legs and made my way back toward the house, dragging its long ears in the dust. "What the hell kind of rabbit is that?" was Marta's greeting as she stood in the patio, having been alerted by the sound of the shot reverberating around the lake. "*Mara, mara*," corrected Juan, "It's a hare, not a rabbit." I knew that back in Britain, hare was considered a rare delicacy, the kind of thing that highbrow chefs delighted in. Marta, however, was not impressed. "I'm not going to eat that," she stated bluntly. Juan seemed less certain: "I think the old people used to eat them. I'll ask my dad." I seemed to remember something about leaving hares to hang for a few days before cooking them, so in the end we nailed it to the outside of the door, just out of reach of the dogs and cats patrolling the patio.

Of course, it then rained. The bedraggled hare seemed even less appetizing the next morning, and even Mateo wouldn't touch it. In the end, the poor creature was dismembered by Juan, boiled in water, and given to the dogs, who immediately took the pieces away to eat in the solitude that starving dogs with food will always seek.

What was it about hunting that gripped me so? It wasn't eating the game, nor the satisfaction of the kill. I think it was a feeling of being connected to the world in a way that I wasn't when I simply walked through it. Gun in hand, even the trees seemed to take notice, and the breeze felt as if it were a breath in my ear. The world became both alive and responsive, where before it had seemed flat and cold. I no longer just wandered: I now wandered with a purpose, with a goal. But the hare's sad demise awoke in me the realization of a particular kind of failure, the strange and perverse need to destroy something in order to have a relation with it, to wield the power of death over it for it to come truly alive.

There's a photo of me from that time, with a baseball cap and a dusty, ripped Carhartt jacket, sitting on a log with my goddaughter

Alejandra on my knee. Across my other knee lies my gun, and in Alejandra's hands is a male California quail, its black crest flopping over its black-and-white face. She must be three, maybe four, and is smiling at the dead bird in her hands. And I am smiling at her. The sunlight falls upon us from above. That quail was the last creature I shot, with the last cartridge in the box. The desire to hunt seems to have left me then, for now it seemed that I had done enough to get the world's attention; that it saw me and wrapped itself around me, and that all would be well. I wrapped the gun back into its potato sack and placed it carefully under my bed.

* * *

Most of the people around the lake were Catholic by default. Some truly embraced the faith, while others had simply passed through the church on the four important occasions that marked the stages of the life cycle—baptism, first communion, marriage, and death. The area had been missionized a hundred years earlier by Bavarian Capuchins, fierce, unyielding men with long gray beards that people remember to this day. They protected the people from the worst of the Chilean land usurpations, but at a price: the yielding of the right to define the parameters of the world, an insistence on drawing an impermeable line between mutually exclusive domains of "Man" and "Nature." The Capuchins were not tolerant people, yet they did acknowledge at least some aspects of Mapuche wisdom and even recorded them in dictionaries and other texts, perhaps seeing traces of their own faith rippling and repeated across time and space. In recent years, however, it had seemed to local people as though the Church was in retreat. Only rarely would a priest come out from the port, and the Fijian missionaries who had once lived next to the school and been marveled at for the deep blackness of their skin were long gone.

Into this vacuum came "the evangelicals," from a variety of Pentecostal churches ranging in scale from the international Kingdom of God, with its global congregation of millions, to an out-shed attached to a man's barn, with a congregation of three. These new churches seemed to hate all things Mapuche, while at the same time being more Mapuche than the Catholic church had ever been. Their congregants were strictly prohibited from attending any traditional rituals, all of which were dismissed as "demonic," from the *ngillatun* fertility ritual to the ritualized sport of *palin*. They were prohibited, too, from drinking alcohol, in many ways a key component of Mapuche sociality. Thus, converting to belong to one of these churches could be equated to a purposeful withdrawal from the mainstream of society. These were the people I didn't see, couldn't name, didn't recognize. Yet at the same time, these were often the people who were the most Mapuche, whom local people would describe as the most *mapuchado*: those with the least competency in Spanish and the greatest fear of witchcraft. It was telling that while the Catholic Mass was always in Spanish, the evangelical gatherings were frequently held in Mapudungun. Likewise, the Catholic Church was reluctant to engage with discourses of witches and witchcraft. Perhaps its own dismissal of so much preconquest Indigenous culture as somehow satanic had stained the topic with a sense of embarrassment or, at the very least, a lack of tact. When people went to the priest with problems of witchcraft, he would tell them to reconcile with their neighbor and then go to the doctor. The evangelical churches, however, dealt with witches head-on, fully open to the inevitability of their existence in the most literal of terms. There were endless exorcisms, banging of drums, all-night prayer meetings: basically all of the central elements of traditional Mapuche shamanism, but in the name of Christ and the kingdom to come.

Despite the theological chasm between the Catholic and evangelical churches, people's adherence to one or the other was frequently fluid. While some people were firmly and permanently embedded in one camp or the other, the majority oscillated, depending on life's needs: a neighbor who'd been drinking too much became evangelical for a few months until he felt better; another neighbor sought out the evangelicals after the priest had refused to curse the witch who'd been attacking her at night, but returned to the Catholic Church once the evangelicals had taken this spiritual revenge on her behalf. My friend Felipe was one of those who shifted denomination on a fairly regular basis. He was a big man—I couldn't reach my arms around him when we embraced—but also very poor, living in a tiny house on the island with his elderly wife. Ironically, I'd met him while drinking wine, but now I would occasionally drop in on him to sip *mate* tea through a metal straw and practice my pitiful Mapudungun. He was one of very few people who would actually correct the mistakes I made or confess that he hadn't understood a word that I'd said.

I'm not sure whether it was out of interest or obligation, but Felipe would often turn our conversations to matters of theology; in particular, queries and theories concerning the Old Testament account of the creation of the world and its peopling. Like many others before him, he often tried to draw parallels between the Mapuche narratives of such events and those presented in the Bible. In particular, he was drawn to the great flood, an inundation paralleled in the Mapuche story of Treng-Treng and Kai-Kai, the battle between two great primordial serpents that caused the sea to rise and flood the land. One evening Felipe got his Bible down off the shelf and gave it to me as a gift. It was just the New Testament and it was written in Mapudungun, the fruit of nine years of labor by the American evangelical Bible-translation organization, the Summer Institute of Linguistics. Despite being fluent speakers, almost nobody at the lake knew how to read or write in Mapudungun, so Felipe and I were confronted with a text that neither one of us could read. He didn't own a Bible in Spanish. He had learned its stories and messages orally, from the pastor at the evangelical gatherings he attended. Nevertheless, he gave me this book, so central to his life and his identity. I have it still and every so often I get it off the shelf and leaf through it, seeing if I can make out any of the words. Only recently did I discover Felipe's signature inside the front cover, a black line crawling slowly across the page at an oblique angle to his faith.

Juan's brother Emilio was another evangelical, but one who, unlike most, was firmly and staunchly committed to the new faith and had been so for decades, since its very first arrival at the shores of the lake. Although he lived just up the hill from me, less than half a mile away, I rarely saw him. A vicious pack of dogs prevented me from ever approaching his house too closely. Still, he would always greet me when he saw me, and on one occasion he gave me a small plastic tub of the perfumed honey he produced in hives hidden down in the gully. Emilio had a jet-black horse—a fast horse, a beautiful horse, some said a witch's horse—that held Emilio in its thrall. Everybody wanted to enter Emilio's horse in the occasional races along the beach, where people bet eye-wateringly large sums of money. But of course, Emilio was having none of that. Gambling was clearly the work of the Devil, and the wine that was copiously drunk at these races just another step on the path to damnation. He would never even put the horse into a gallop for sheer joy; instead, he let it run wild, keeping itself plump on other people's pastures, and he saddled it just once a week for a slow ambling walk to an evangelical church by the sea.

This was all too much for Mateo. The beauty of the mare's form, its coiled strength, its black so black it was blue, could not be resisted forever. One autumn morning over breakfast, we glimpsed her silent dark shape through the open door as she slipped across Juan and Marta's patio, with my own mare Quintrala close behind, their sharp breaths pushing white blasts of steam into the cold of the morning. "Let's race," said Mateo. This didn't seem to me like a particularly good idea, but I guess I, too, was smitten by the black mare's beauty. Mateo grabbed a small handful of oats, a short blue rope, and a bright pink potato sack, and we quietly left the house in pursuit. The oats were enough to capture the two mares' interest, and as they nosed Mateo's hand, his other hand slipped the rope delicately around the black mare's neck.

He had a technique for tying a makeshift halter that would just about
let you ride a well-tempered horse. The black mare didn't resist, but
I could sense something in her eye, in the toss of her head, that to
me at least indicated that she was somewhat affronted by the whole
situation. Beauty is, as Rilke once said, the first step on the road to
terror, but in this case the full terror was yet to reveal itself. She didn't
struggle when Mateo sprawled across her and swung his leg around
to mount her, stuffing the potato sack underneath as a kind of temporary horse blanket. I mounted my own mare, in much the same fashion, but without the potato sack and with a bona fide bridle and reins.

We rode the horses down to the narrow strip of meadow that separated the trees from the reedbeds of the lake. Flocks of small birds
lifted from the ground as we approached. "A case of beer" was the
wager Mateo proposed. I neither agreed nor disagreed, knowing full
well that he'd never buy it even if I won. I was in fact fairly confident that he would not win, not through any great belief in my own
horse or my limited skills as a jockey, but because I had noticed the
black mare's alertness, the flicking of her ears, her brief snorts in the
still-cold morning air, the odd flick of a hoof. There was no starter,
no line; we just waited until the two horses were more or less facing in the same direction along the lakeshore, and then we set off.
We hadn't even gone thirty yards before the black mare dipped her
shoulder, changed the direction of her gallop by the slightest margin,
and let Mateo soar off her back to land, beached, on top of a broad
clump of thick reeds, the blue rope somehow still in his hand, unraveled, undone. We watched as the mare continued her gallop up the
slope and away through the woods, the pink potato sack slipping off
among the trees. Mateo cursed her all the way home, limping along
as I rode beside him.

That horse must now be long dead. Emilio I never see, even on my
visits to the lake. Yet I often wonder about those two—how a life that
to me seemed so dry, so perversely deprived of all color and warmth,
so overdetermined by strictness and self-control, could come to be

shared with an entity of such innate and intrinsic wildness, a terrible beauty like the roar of the ocean to a drowning man.

*   *   *

There are some stories that you like to tell, that make people laugh or that paint you, perhaps with a calculated air of humility, in a good light. And there are of course others that you don't tell, out of shame or guilt, but they are stories nonetheless and they persist in your memory, strange objects like lozenges for your thoughts to suck on on sleepless nights. The story of how I killed a dog is one such story.

A man died. To be honest, I can't remember his name or how he died. He was my friend Eduvino's elder brother and I'd met him a few times over on the island, working or drinking. He was a very cheerful, friendly man in late middle age, quite short and very skinny. He'd been single all his life. Anyway, the man died, and as I'd known him, and as I was a friend of Eduvino, and because I supposed that this was the kind of thing anthropologists should do, I rode over to the island for the wake, known in Mapudungun as *umawtun*.

Mapuche wakes are not much different from wakes elsewhere in the world; people sit around accompanying the dead person through the night, before the person is buried. People drink and people cry. It was already nighttime by the time I reached the house of Eduvino's parents, both of them then still alive (and both now dead). It was a somewhat strange house in comparison to the other houses around, built in an L-shape out of heavy, rough-hewn timber boards. One wing of the house was almost like a barn, a large open space with a high roof and a small kitchen at one end. It was in here that the corpse was laid, and a large number of people were seated around all four sides of the room. I'm not sure whether this was in the days before electricity came to the lake, or whether it had already come and simply not reached Eduvino's parents' house, but there were kerosene lamps hanging from the rafters at either end of the room. The light they threw was a smudged yellow and barely penetrated the darkness. People were talking quietly among themselves, several with glass bottles at their feet, filled with red wine. A few people turned and looked a bit surprised to see a white person enter such a place, so far from the port and the city, so far from the world of the *winka*, the world of the whites. Most, however, already knew me or at least recognized me and simply nodded an acknowledgment of my presence.

Eduvino seemed happy that I'd come. He smiled, thanked me, and handed me a bottle brimming with wine and a glass. He shuffled an old, slightly drunk man along a bench to make space for me to sit down before he moved off to see to other guests. It took me a few minutes to realize that the man he had displaced for me was Francisco, Eduvino's own father and the father of the dead man lying in the center of the room. Francisco, like his sons, was always smiling, and even tonight he was smiling, although tears ran down his cheeks as he smiled. He must have been in his eighties at that time, and he died a couple of years later; I would later sit on this same bench at his wake. Francisco didn't want to talk about his son or about death, but rather about me or, more specifically, about life in Britain. Was it true that Britain had its own Mapuche people? If not, who were the poor people? Who lived in the countryside and grew stuff? Was it they who had taught me to speak Mapudungun? The idea that "every country has its own Mapuche people" continues to be widespread, especially among older people in more rural areas. I was never quite sure whether or not to correct people as I was never quite sure exactly what they meant by "Mapuche"—a defined ethnic group? a universal social category? a global rural proletariat? This particular night, I really didn't know what to think or say, so I tried to steer the conversation back to the dead man lying in front of us, hat on his chest, candles at his feet. But Francisco wasn't interested, whether through grief, annoyance, or boredom, I don't know; this evening he wanted to understand the world of the whites, a world that only coheres into being when you are one of those excluded from all it promises.

We drank as we talked, and the glasses circled around in their perpetual counterclockwise motion as men took it in turns to serve the collected mourners from their bottles. Women came in, but then quickly disappeared into the kitchen and on to whatever lay beyond. Some people now seemed to have carafes of cider in addition to the wine, and it wasn't long before the ambient volume increased as voices were raised. Francisco remained on a level plane, smiling and crying— maybe there's no other response when your child dies, no matter how old or how wayward. The bodies filling the room started to raise not only the volume, but the temperature, and I could feel the drink going to my head. Eduvino's wife, Ignacia, tapped me on the shoulder at one point and called Francisco and me through to the kitchen, but Francisco waved her away. I, however, was grateful for the chance to escape and followed Ignacia to the small back room where she, Eduvino, and Eduvino's mother were eating a roast of what looked like lamb. "No, it's mutton," corrected Eduvino, "one of the dogs turned wild and savaged her, so we've no choice but to eat her now. It's still good." The meat was indeed good, but there was no joy as we ate it, the loss of the ewe compounding the loss of a brother, a son. It struck me as strange how the mortality of men and sheep always seems to go hand in hand.

After we'd finished eating, I asked Eduvino whose dog had been responsible, wondering if he'd try and recoup some of his loss. "It was my own dog, the gray one," he replied sadly. "He's out there now, just beyond the well." I wondered what he meant: was the dog still at large, dismembering and devouring sheep; or was it dead, awaiting disposal? I couldn't help but ask. "I threw a log at him and broke his back, he's out there still." I didn't quite know what to think or do, but found myself slowly getting to my feet and making my way to the back door. "Where are you going?" asked Ignacia. "You can't leave a dog like that," I said, perhaps sounding a bit more indignant than I intended. She just shrugged, and Eduvino, like his father, just kept smiling and crying.

I went out into the cool night air, and its coolness immediately entered me and made me aware of the alcohol running through me. It seemed to carry with it a calmness and an air of inevitability that wrapped itself around me as I walked over to a pile of split logs to collect the axe. It was dark, the sky a deep gray; no moon, no stars. Despite the darkness, I found the dog without difficulty, in the long grass behind the well. At first I thought it was already dead; it seemed not to be moving at all, but then I noticed the slightest of rises in its chest. I put my hand to its side and despite the wild flickering of its eyes, there was no movement in its body. I stepped back and without hesitation raised the axe, then brought its blunt side crashing down on the dog's head, twice in quick succession. Wiping the axe off in the grass, I felt the cool air again blowing against my cheek. I came to the back door and Ignacia gave me a bowl of water to wash the blood off my hands and face. Nobody said a word when I came in and sat down.

To this day, I persuade myself that I did the right thing: I put a suffering animal with no hope of recovery out of its misery. But in my heart I know that that is only half the story, a moral justification that sits seamlessly on top of something much darker and more fearful, the strange elation I felt at taking a life, being the witch who presides over and administers death. I felt this elation and I feared it.

The strange surge of power soon faded and I sat once again next to the body of that strange man and thought of the body I'd left outside; I was crying, but also smiling.

*   *   *

Esteban and I used to talk occasionally about making a film together. Its premise was simple: he would walk around the woods and gullies bordering his fields and talk in Mapudungun about all of the plants he encountered and his relationship with them. The plants would be the characters of our film, their personalities, their quirks, their traits all made visible for the imagined viewer. There would be no plot, no narrative as such, just a glimpse into other lives, into another society.

We never ended up making the film; for a start, neither of us knew how to, and as a result both of us soon moved our attention to other things. But what remained with me was just how simple, easy, and even friendly Esteban's relationships with plants were and how obvious it seemed to him that this would be the case. He would apologize to trees before cutting them down, would mumble a few words to each little potato seed before slipping it into the soil and a few more to the golden stalks of wheat before reaping them. Esteban was not alone in this regard. In Mapuche life, the intimate relationships of give-and-take with plants, animals, and places are not fundamentally different from those with other people; they follow the same basic format of a hospitality that must be reciprocated and whose reciprocation will in turn be reciprocated, leading to an infinite, flowing relationship of unceasing exchange, of give-and-take.

Life for the people I knew was made possible and sustained by relationships. In fact, life *was* relationships. Sometimes Mapuche people talk of *itrofill mongen,* which you might translate as "all of the varieties of life" or "all of the species that make up life." To produce something was simply to enter into relationships with this dazzling variety of the many forms that life took, each in itself a part of the endless flow of force. A corollary of this social philosophy is that nothing, not even what we might think of as crude, raw material substances, can stand outside the sphere of social relations. And a key consequence of this, as the Brazilian anthropologist Eduardo Viveiros de Castro once pointed out, is that the typical Western understanding of production as an act of human manipulation and transformation of raw material, of something active acting on something passive, is alien to Indigenous ways of thinking. It is always a social exchange of one kind or another that brings new entities into being: to create is to relate is to create is to relate, and so on ad infinitum.

The word *kümeche* refers to one of the aspects of personhood that Mapuche people strive to embrace and embody. While *che* means "true person" and *küme* simply means "good," in this context it refers to much more than that. *Kümeche* is sometimes translated as "rich person," but that isn't strictly accurate, either. For a person can be rich without being good; in fact, as we saw above, the figure of the *witranalwe*—the demon bodyguard wrought from bones in occult rituals—turns out to ultimately be a kind of Faustian bargain: the rich are rich precisely because they are *not* good, because they don't share, because they seek not to exchange but to hoard and accumulate. A more accurate translation of *kümeche* would be "generous person," somebody who gives to all, who shares with all, whose hospitality embraces everybody. But even this translation of *kümeche* perhaps obscures why this generosity is so important in Mapuche thought, for it is neither the material goods themselves nor the single act of giving alone that is impotant. What *kümeche* really refers to is the person who distributes, who keeps the endless cycles of exchanges flowing, for this is what life is: the never-ending flow of abundance that ties all things together.

It is the witch who tries to shatter these cycles that constitute life. Through the witch's perverse violence, the flow of life is reversed and blocked. In the witch's actions, those relationships that should be productive, open-ended, and flowing become cut short, dried-up, and destroyed. To learn to be *kümeche* is to stand against the witch and learn to give and receive, to open oneself up to the wonder of all things. In the wake of the witch's destruction, the *kümeche* rebuilds, reintegrates, and reimagines the endless flow of relationships that constitute life. This is not a lesson that we learn once and can then forget; we have to relearn it every day, every waking moment. For the witch is always there, within us, waiting, biding its time.

ii

clown

Who is the clown? The clown is the one who takes what should only be given. This is another way of saying that they cannot see love. It is love through which people satisfy their bodies and through their bodies that love is given. Their bodies wasted in the fields or the cities to provide food and drink for others; their bodies given at night to each other to satisfy desires and to keep the chain of love flowing.

The clown does not see this, does not understand. They snatch the food from the plate, unbidden. They grope and grasp the bodies, uninvited. Where there is love, they see but flesh. Mapuche people point their fingers at the clown, they dress up and perform them, acting temporarily as if there were no love, no culture, no right and no wrong. These clowns make us laugh, but they warn us, too, of the absurdity of a life without love, a base life reduced to the consumption of calories and the diffusion of genes.

How easy it is, now more than ever, to be the clown. To fulfill our desires without loving or being loved, without coming face to face with another; to imagine ourselves as self-sufficient, as already complete. The clowns remind us, their lives of poverty and violence a warning to turn back to love, to cede the fulfillment of our desires to others and in turn to fulfill those desires in others through our love for them.

*   *   *

45

Many years ago, bored with writing field notes, I tried to write a poem. The poem was to be about a man called Jerónimo, a frequent visitor to Juan and Marta's house. I can't remember anything of the poem; I suspect I never finished it. But I do remember thinking that there was something about Jerónimo that evoked a literary character, compelled an artistic response of some kind or other. Why I thought that, I don't really know, but for some reason I think it still. Maybe it's because he always seemed to have only one foot in our world, with the other somewhere beyond; and no matter how ludicrous the situation in which he found himself, no matter how humiliating, he always seemed to stare head-on at the inevitability of tragedy. The most striking thing about him physically was his nose, flattened against one side of his face in some brawl several years previously, during his Santiago years. Many of the people I knew at the lake had spent time in their youth in Santiago, and some had better luck there than others. Many stayed, but many returned home to the south. The precise story of Jerónimo's nose was never fully revealed; people would speculate, and Jerónimo would just smile and nod. He was a drinker, a heavy drinker, and I would often hear him knocking at my window just before dawn, looking for someone to drink with. So ingrained was the Mapuche injunction against serving oneself that the men who suffered from alcoholism would wander from homestead to homestead, a carton clutched under their arm, looking for somebody to give it to and thus be able to drink with. When drunk, Jerónimo became quiet and pensive, never violent.

One day, Jerónimo asked me to become his godfather. For some reason, he'd slipped through the net of confirmation, but the catechists from the port had finally caught up with him, and he was being confirmed as an adult. I declined his request, too confused by the strange dynamic of being a godfather to somebody at least two decades older than myself. Now, years later, I regret that decision, having come to understand that for Jerónimo godfatherhood was a way of bridging social chasms, trying to equalize power relations to a certain degree. He understood that we were from different worlds, but through his request hoped to lay a foundation upon which a bridge between us could be built.

Jerónimo was a clown, both figuratively and literally. He would clown around, and his drinking led him into all kinds of ludicrous situations that he met with corresponding ludicrousness, miming, mimicking, performing, until he inevitably went too far and would be thrown out into the mud. But Jerónimo was also *koyong*, a ritual clown central to the great *ngillatun* fertility ritual and the highly ritualized sport of *palin*. He would don a mask, mount a wooden horse, stuff straw into his clothes, and gallop up and down the ranks of dancers, screaming, stealing, groping, cursing, reminding us all of what we were not. One could never quite tell where the boundaries of his ritual performance began and ended: what was an act, what was not.

They say that clowns always live in poverty, must always suffer, and must always die before their time. Jerónimo, it turned out, was no different. At the end of last year, a friend forwarded me a story from the online version of the local newspaper. There was a grainy photo of a man I recognized but couldn't quite place, being led into a courthouse in handcuffs by two policemen. A murder had taken place at the lake. This time, an elderly man had been stabbed to death while drinking. Through the various euphemisms that saturated the article, I thought I could deduce that it was a drunken argument that had exploded into violence. I eventually recognized the man in the photo as Motrilu, a man who was, if not exactly mute, very limited in his communicative capabilities.

Motrilu belonged to one of the very last families at the lake that not only didn't, but couldn't, speak Spanish. The existence of monolingual speakers of Mapudungun is a phenomenon that most Chileans, even those who work directly on issues relating to Mapuche people, refuse to believe exists in the twenty-first century. The idea that people born and raised on supposedly Chilean soil could be so socially and culturally remote from the mainstream of Chilean national culture remains unthinkable to them. Then, when actually confronted with the concrete reality of these people, they view their monolingualism as some kind of shocking pathology that needs fixing, a lacuna that needs filling. Not surprisingly, they don't see the monolingual Spanish speakers who make up the vast majority of Chile's population in the same light. It's certainly true that these days, families that speak solely Mapudungun are few and far between, but they exist nonetheless. Motrilu's mother, Lucia, was very shy and reclusive. Despite her fair skin and light hazel eyes, she spoke not a word of Spanish. People thought she must be a descendant of one of the European passengers of the *Joven Daniel*, a ship that wrecked off the coast of Inalafken in the nineteenth century and whose female survivors married local Mapuche men. Lucia was a talented weaver, and I still have a *makuiñ* that she wove, a poncho of natural, undyed wool, so thick that neither light nor water can penetrate it. It is brown, beige, and gray, and each stripe of color merges into the next like a melancholy rainbow. Lucia's two children were Sofia and Motrilu, neither of whom spoke much, if at all, and both of whom seemed somewhat nervous of people, reluctant to engage.

Motrilu must have been about the same age as me, and I would often bump into him either at work parties, football tournaments, or just rambling along the road. He would smile shyly behind his long black hair, maybe raise a hand, but rarely speak. When people were drinking, they'd get him drunk and try to bait him with predictably crude jokes about his sister. He would just smile and wave them away, his large frame seeming so small and insufficient against the barrage of all that laughter. After I was sent the newspaper clipping, I was told that something inside Motrilu had finally snapped and that he had killed Jerónimo in a violent and sustained attack, stabbing him multiple times. As to why he did it, nobody seemed to know. But that Jerónimo, the clown, would die in such a way seemed to surprise no one.

There is a dark side to life and when you're far from home, it can be harder to see, easier to ignore, more difficult to pinpoint. It was these people, people like Jerónimo and Motrilu, people who were dismissed by their neighbors as *demasiado mapuchado*, "too Mapuche," who made me laugh, who made me happy and bought me drinks. There was so much that I couldn't see, or rather didn't want to see: that for all the laughter, the joke had long since ceased to be funny, that those who fell through the webs constructed of love and care would fall hard. Motrilu and Jerónimo were both born into poverty, lived in poverty, and one will most likely follow the other to die in poverty—the treasures they held, the beauty of them, their language, and their stories dismissed and disregarded by the same fickle history that condemned them to such poverty in the first place.

*   *   *

One evening I danced in the fire; not intentionally, but by accident. Sparks flew up around me and surrounded me like an orange halo. The rubber soles of my shoes started to melt, my feet uncomfortably warm. People were starting to stare, and a child was sent to pull me out of the flames, no adult wanting to taint themselves with the embarrassment of a drunken *winka*, a white person, dancing alone in a fire. What can I say? I was drunk and lonely, maybe drunk on loneliness. I was surrounded by people who cared for me, who called me nephew and whom I called uncle or auntie, and whom I, too, cared for. But that was not enough; I needed love of the romantic kind as well. I had convinced myself that I was in love with one particular woman, about my age, who had returned from the city to look after an aging grandmother on the island. She was polite and friendly, and in her I could see the realization of a dream of being settled somewhere, with someone. I could be quite happy, I told myself, with a little house at the lake's edge, a nice horse, and a growing family. I suspect that even then I probably realized there was something so profoundly naïve and misplaced about this dream that I repeatedly sabotaged any possibility of it ever actually happening. Maybe that's why that evening I drank so much and so quickly.

It was the party following a football tournament, or perhaps it was a party to celebrate the new community hall; I can't remember. It was near the small football pitch on old Renato's land, although Renato himself was not in attendance, bedridden because he had plowed through a wasps' nest and received more than forty stings. We'd spent most of the day building the ramadas, the makeshift shelters from which we could sell wine and beer and thus hopefully make some profit for the community funds. And there was a larger ramada at the end of the open, rectangular space, built to house the live music, a local band of young men playing slightly warped versions of the Mexican *ranchera* country music that has such a deep hold on the rural Chilean imagination. These versions always struck me as so utterly different from their original Mexican counterparts, although I could never quite pinpoint why. While the original songs appeared truly epic, opening out onto broad horizons of grandeur, I always heard their rural Chilean versions as domestic, claustrophobic, inward-looking.

Still, the relentless rhythm of the music and the strange, almost falsetto-like singing took hold of me. I ordered carton after carton of wine, and stumbled from corner to corner of the large rectangle formed by the shelters looking for somebody to give it to and thus share with. This was still early in the evening, and at this stage most people there were, like myself, meant to be acting as hosts for the event that was yet to get truly underway. They were therefore, if not exactly abstaining from drinking, at least meant to be drinking in moderation. Would that I could have had the same restraint! More and more people started to arrive, and the next time I turned my attention away from the circulating glass in front of me, the night had arrived, the sky turned black.

I was looking out for this young woman, the one on whom I had pinned my future by the lake. And eventually she arrived, polite and smiling as always. Nobody was dancing, but yet I asked her to dance. She hesitated, perhaps out of kindness, not sure whether it was crueler to flat-out reject me or to allow the delusional spectacle to roll on. Unfortunately, she went for the latter, and with one arm around her waist and another holding her hand, I moved her to the music, into the space in front of the band. The singer paused to glance in my direction, barely supressing a laugh, before launching into the ever-popular *Paloma Blanca*. I couldn't keep the rhythm; I could barely move my body in any controlled fashion. The only people we'd inspired to join us in the dancing were middle-aged bachelors, also drunk too soon and dancing by themselves in the white light of the half-moon and the red light of the small fires that people had lit around the ramadas to heat water or to roast bits of chicken. As the song ended, my chosen one slipped away with the greatest delicacy, back to the man who it later transpired was her boyfriend, fiancé even, although they never did marry.

I didn't quite know what to do with myself, so I kept dancing, alone and out of time. The pulse of the music lifted my head as it closed my eyes. An empty glass was somehow still in my hand. I spun and stepped and glided around the space, bumping into other dancers, until I centered myself and, rather than moving horizontally, focused on a kind of vertical bobbing, the like of which I doubt had ever been seen before or since. It was at this stage that I felt a tug on my sleeve—a child—telling me that it was time to go home. Mapuche people often avoid confrontations with drunk people by getting a child to intervene, knowing that a child won't provoke aggression and cannot easily be denied. I was led quietly away by this child, past the ramadas, to the stumbling, falling walk home. The next day, I rode over to the house of the young woman's grandmother on the island, to apologize as best I could for the humiliation I had brought down upon both of us. She stood there, as polite and smiling as ever, accepting my apology with good grace and even a laugh.

I still feel the humiliation of this event twenty years later. I look around the reading room of the National Library of Scotland, where I'm writing, to see whether anybody else has seen my face go red, suspecting that shame still lingers like an indelible aura around me. If truth be told, that was neither the first nor the last time that the overlap of loneliness, alcohol, and a general sense of being unmoored in this world would lead me to ever more spectacular scenes of humiliation, both private and public. This is what clowns do: they confuse means and ends, content and form, the body for the soul and the soul for the body. I was at least in the right trade; anthropologists are professional clowns, gaining purchase in our inability to understand desire, to always mistake it for something else: politics, calories, genes.

*   *   *

Just as there are different ways to fail, there are different ways to fall off horses. Over my years at the lake, I experienced quite a few of them. Horses were, until relatively recently, ubiquitous in Mapuche life. Before the bridge over the far arm of the lake was constructed, most men and some women would travel to the port on horseback, a four-hour ride along the beach. (Horses were also a valuable source of meat and, indeed, continue to be so in many Mapuche communities elsewhere in Chile and Argentina—a source of disgust to many white Chileans.) Many Mapuche rituals, such as the *ngillatun* fertility ritual and the traditional *eluwun* funerals, require great circuits of galloping horsemen, cleansing the ritual space of any malevolent beings that might be present. And, as in many parts of the world, horses came to be an extension of the masculine person, both the end and the means of a manly life. They enabled men to partake in social life, to travel far from their natal communities, to find wives and friends or other riches. My friend Esteban's grandfather once rode from the lake at the shores of the Pacific all the way across an entire continent to the Atlantic. And historically, it was the Mapuche people's embracing of the horse that provided the foundation for their immense political and territorial power throughout the eighteenth and nineteenth centuries, a source of great value, military strength, and unprecedented mobility. Some say that the Argentine figure of the *gaucho* comes from the Mapuche word *kawchu*, "bachelor": the unmarried Mapuche men roaming the Cordillera and pampas on horseback seeking riches and adventure.

By the time I arrived at the lake in the nineties, the heyday of horses was already coming to an end. Increasing pressure on the land meant less space to keep horses and to grow the oats they needed to survive the winter. Improved public transportation, with a daily bus service, further reduced their practical importance. Nevertheless, such is the centrality of horses to Mapuche identity that many homesteads still kept one or two, and horse racing continued to be an obsession for many. Esteban was particularly passionate about horses, owning three, breeding them, and offering veterinary assistance to other horse owners. I was already somewhat familiar with horses before arriving at the lake, but now they were to become a major part of my daily life. I would regularly ride out with Esteban on various errands, or just to get to know the land. I acquired a handsome pair of leather boots and a fearsome pair of spurs. In Chile, people use wooden saddles accompanied by elaborately carved wooden stirrups, all kept in place by a pair of cinch belts around the horse's belly. At the zenith of Mapuche political power in the nineteenth century, an entire art form had built up around the creation of ornate silver horse tack. It was such silver bits and bridles that formed the "buried treasure" of many stories.

The first rule of riding on one of these wooden saddles is that your behind should never leave contact with the saddle. The moment it does, you're done for. This lesson was learned the hard way. Esteban's son-in-law, Kiko, a keen *huaso*—the traditional Chilean cowboy—was visiting from the port with a stocky chestnut mare that he was training for the next rodeo. He invited me to have a try riding her, and with perhaps a touch too much confidence I agreed. The wry smile on both his and Esteban's faces should probably have warned me. I mounted the horse and eased her into a gentle trot, easing my weight off the saddle in time with the horse's strides in what is known as posting in the European style that I'd been taught. However, the second my backside left the saddle, the mare bolted forward into a flat gallop. Once you're up out of the saddle, under those conditions, it's almost impossible to get back down, and I was helpless as the horse steered into a wire fence. I was thrown straight over the fence into the relative cushioning of a recently plowed field, my face narrowly missing the barbed wire as I sailed over it. Kiko and Esteban rushed over, immediately checking the chest and flanks of the horse, while I sat humiliated and dazed in the mud. The horse had actually managed to halt before hitting the fence, so she was unhurt and turned toward me with what I interpreted as a haughty gaze.

This happened in one of my first months at the lake, and I can't deny that my confidence with horses was somewhat dented by it. Nevertheless, avoiding horses wasn't really an option there; they are the source of a man's freedom, the means by which he can go out into the world and bring it to heel. Some older women were renowned as great horsewomen; indeed, Esteban's mother, long deceased, had been known to have a gift with horses, calming them with quiet words and soft caresses as they learned to take a saddle and be mounted. Now, however, one almost never saw women on horseback. Why this was, I'm not quite sure. But for now, they seemed to be very much part of being a man. Given that a certain kind of masculinity was what I aspired to back then, the thought of strutting around in cowboy boots, getting on and off horses, conquering the world, had a deep hold on my psyche. I couldn't get over how great my spurs sounded as they jangled across the rough-hewn wooden floors. It seemed that my aspirations toward masculinity had never really evolved beyond the huge, omnipresent Marlboro man billboards at the end of the city street where I was raised, and if Marlboro cigarettes had been available at the lake, I'm sure I would have started smoking them.

The need and desire to ride eventually took me out once more. On this occasion, I at least got a little further than the end of Esteban's driveway before falling. This fall, however, was even more humiliating than the first, primarily because the horse wasn't actually moving when I fell off it. Esteban and I had ridden for a couple of hours southwest to Inalafken, a cluster of reservations next to the Pacific. And while the isthmus's boundary with the ocean was marked by great sea cliffs, the coast at Inalafken descended into a broad, flat expanse of sand. Over the years, various people had tried to set up tourist businesses here of one kind or another. One friend had constructed a large-scale *ruka*, the traditional Mapuche longhouse, offering a bar and food within. Others had tried a small campsite, and the odd kiosk or two stood abandoned along the stretch of beach nearest the road. Tourism was the great hope of many in the area; development officers in the regional capital believed that the combination of "traditional Indigenous culture" and the unspoiled sandy beaches would tempt tourists from elsewhere in Chile and beyond. The tourists, however, never came. In all my years at the lake, I don't think I saw even one. These days, the odd trickle of curious Germans and Americans does apparently occasionally arrive, just enough to prevent the hope from being completely extinguished, but never in anywhere near the numbers required to create a reliable and sustainable source of income. Most tourists to the south are magnetically drawn to the spectacular inland beauty of the lakes and mountains of the Cordillera, not the windswept, abject poverty of the coast.

Thus, the occasional customers who did frequent the kiosks in Inalafken were not tourists but rather local Mapuche families spending a day at the beach. This wouldn't have been a problem for the fledgling tourist businesses if it hadn't been for the fact that these families nearly always brought their own food with them, the women setting up little fires for their meat and *mate* tea. They did, however, at least buy drinks. And that was why Esteban and I had ridden to Inalafken: to see the great ocean and maybe have a drink or two. I'd like to claim that my fall occurred after a lengthy drinking session, but in fact, it occurred before we'd even arrived. We'd dismounted briefly to talk to a man about some vaccine or other, and to allow the horses a quick drink from a small pool.

The construction of the wooden saddles, and the relative looseness with which the cinch belts are tied, means that you can't dally in getting your leg over the horse and into the far stirrup. If you pause with all of your weight in the near stirrup, the saddle will simply slide around and under the horse's belly. That very thing had happened to me earlier that morning, and I'd had to dismount and retie the cinch straps while Esteban groaned with impatience in the background. This time, therefore, with that in mind, I stepped into the near stirrup and, in one explosive movement, threw all of my weight upwards. The result was that I flew neatly over the saddle and, without making any contact with the horse at all, landed on my face on the far side. Fortunately, we were already in the dunes next to the beach, so my face met sand rather than gravel. The real pain, of course, was to my pride. This incident happened more than twenty-five years ago, but when I saw Esteban last year, he was laughing about it still.

Once I'd recovered from the fall and Esteban had more or less recovered from laughing, we rode on to the long, broad strip of reddish-brown sand to give the horses a run. We removed the saddles from the horses, leaving them wearing just the intricately woven saddle blankets, and Esteban hopped back on and spurred each horse in turn into a flat-out gallop. There's a whole series of dark arts and arcane wisdom concerned with preparing horses for a race; the phase of the moon, the setting of the sun, even the ripeness of the pasture all play a part in strategizing which horse to put into which race and when. And in order to assess each horse's progress, we would utilize the sandy track to put each one through its paces. After a couple of lengths with each horse, Esteban asked me if I would like a try. I can't deny that I felt some trepidation at the thought of galloping bareback across a beach, having managed to crash off a saddled, stationary horse only an hour or two earlier. "Look, what's the worst that could happen?" asked Esteban. Answers like "death" and "paralysis" crossed my mind, but I hoped that the soft sand would offer at least some margin of safety. And once I was on the horse, I realized two things: first, that riding bareback I could feel the horse's motion and the rate of its strides, and second, that my legs were just about long enough to clamp themselves around the horse's midriff. I galloped up and down the beach feeling as secure as a kid on a tricycle. From that day forth, I only ever rode bareback; my heavy wooden saddle was left to molder in Juan's barn.

The single exception to my bareback commitment occurred a year later and was, not coincidentally, marked by yet another fall, this one even more spectacular than either of the previous two. It was the day of the *ngillatun* fertility ritual to be held at Kura, the colossal sea stack separated from the coast by a few yards of threshing ocean at the foot of the cliffs. This ritual is attended by upwards of two thousand people, with many migrants returning from Santiago or Temuco to participate. Everybody who had a horse would attend on horseback; indeed, the *awun*—the circuits of galloping horses— were a central part of the ritual. I had been preparing carefully over the preceding days: I'd slaughtered a pig the day before, paid Marta to make extra fried bread, and even gotten hold of some *muday*, a slightly fermented traditional corn drink. My shirt was freshly laundered, my spurs shining, and my boots polished. My chestnut mare, Quintrala, was groomed and I was ready to go. Marta observed silently from the doorframe, but when my leg was half-cocked to mount the mare, she yelled "What do you think you're doing? You can't go to a *ngillatun* without a saddle—everyone will think you're poor!" People thinking that you're poor is about as bad as it gets among poor people, and I knew that this would be seen as reflecting on Juan and Marta—that they had a gringo, but only a hopelessly poor one without even a saddle. So, with a significant degree of reluctance, I retrieved the heavy saddle from the barn, blew off the dust, and scrubbed at the mold that was encroaching along the leather cinch.

The ritual itself passed well enough, with no equestrian disasters on my part to speak of. Riding back from Kura in the still-blazing sunshine of early evening, I fell in with a family I knew from the island, the family of a man named Eduardo Díaz. Despite having a Spanish surname, Eduardo was "*bien Mapuchado*," "very Mapuche," a term both derogatory and approving at the same time. Eduardo was riding on horseback alongside his family's oxcart. Wine is prohibited from the ritual hospitality in order to preserve the decorum of this most sacred of Mapuche collective events, but now that the ritual was over, Eduardo had an open carton of red wine partly hidden under his denim jacket, and somehow held a nearly full glass in his other hand. How he was managing to steer his horse, I couldn't quite figure out. He poured me a glass and I drank it as we rode along side by side, our backs to the fat red sun hovering over the ocean to the west. Along the road we seemed to accrue more people, some also on horseback, others on foot, some with their own wine, some without. By the time we had reached the turnoff for the descent to the ford and the island beyond, the group must have numbered around ten or so people. The drinking continued as we came to a stop outside the school. There were a dizzying number of cartons in circulation, people eager to share with guests from other communities, their faces shining with joy at the successful completion of the ritual. The wine and the sun now streaming into my eyes from the west started to fill my head. Having previously come unstuck in these kinds of situations, I had a relatively good instinct for when to withdraw, so when people's attention seemed elsewhere, I discreetly trotted off toward home, as the world spun in circles around me.

The gate that marked the first entry to Juan's fields was simply a slender gray trunk of eucalyptus, resting across two upright posts. It was usually a simple enough task to lift, drop, pass, and replace the trunk without dismounting from the horse. Things were not quite so simple, however, in my current state. The exact sequence of events remains somewhat blurred, but I remember reaching across to grab the pole, yet leaning too far out of the saddle. Without actually falling off the horse, I managed to swing the saddle around the horse's belly ninety degrees so that it and I were parallel to the ground. I somehow then managed to extricate myself from the saddle while propping myself up against the gatepost, and then lower myself to the ground. I really couldn't be doing with fixing the saddle in the now belligerent state the wine had reduced me to. I undid the cinch straps and unceremoniously dumped the saddle in the bushes, to collect the following day. As I walked the horse away from the mess I'd made of the gate, the world opened up before me. I could see across the whole breadth of Chile to the distant volcanoes of the Cordillera, could see the evening star emerge from the dazzling blue, and I could feel a soft breeze accompanying the dying sun at my back. The scene filled me with a sense of power and invincibility. I mounted the horse yet again, this time with nothing but the saddle cloth, grabbed her mane, and squeezed her into a flat-out gallop.

Predictably, to anybody who might have been watching this drama unfold, the horse barely covered ten yards before I was flung off over her shoulder and crumpled with a heavy thud on the grass. Yet the feeling of invincibility had still not deserted me; I got up, dusted myself down, remounted the horse, and again sent her into a full gallop. This time, I only managed about five yards before simply tipping off onto the ground. Perhaps drunkenness was both my downfall and my salvation; my body was so relaxed that it seemed to absorb the hardness of the dry summer ground. I remember the primary source of my dismay being the various stains covering my once-crisp blue shirt: red soil over the sleeves and shoulders, red wine down the front. I mounted up once again and proceeded in a straight line, over the top of the newly plowed hilltop field, toward the house, no longer galloping but walking at a steady pace. And a third time I fell, this time simply slipping exhausted from the horse into the warm embrace of the soft, fresh earth.

On waking the next morning, my whole body hurt: my head from the wine, the rest from the falls. My entire left side was a deep aubergine purple, and tracing my fingers along the lines of my ribs, I could feel something different, something not quite right. The fact that everybody else in the house seemed in an equally bad state brightened my spirits a little bit. And thinking back to the previous evening, I could at least be thankful that my repeated failures had occurred out of sight, thus keeping the humiliation to an individual rather than public scale. I realized that an essential part of my cover-up would be to recover the saddle from beyond the top field before anyone else was up and awake, so I quickly removed the stained clothes of the previous day that I'd slept in and threw on some new ones. But making my way quietly from the house, I was met by the stout figure of my elderly neighbor, Valentina, standing in the patio, my saddle in her arms and a wry smile on her face. "I'm just returning your saddle," she said. "You seem to have dropped it in our hedge last evening, before your 'accidents.'"

*   *   *

Within lies, one often finds truths. The accusation that I was a CIA agent working to infiltrate the Mapuche communities of the lake to further an American imperialist agenda in Chile was one such lie, although it took me years, decades even, to appreciate the truth behind it. Juan and I were part of the social detritus left behind one day by a game of *palin*, a kind of ritualized field hockey, that had been staged in Marta's natal community over on the island. It had been a great day; I'd met lots of friends, made some new ones, learned a lot about the cycles of hospitality that accompany *palin*, and been given lots to eat and drink. Once night had fallen, the games of *palin* stopped and the women of the host community started to pack up their makeshift cooking operations and hitch up the oxcarts to head home. Most of the men stayed on, with the various guests they'd invited from other communities around the lake. A few fires remained burning, casting an orange light over the faces that were present in the moment.

Juan and I were talking with some people from the furthest end of the island, a place where a small wooden bridge connected it to the main road to the port. I knew these people tangentially, and the conversation circled around the usual topics of agricultural prices, who'd died, who was ill, and who might be responsible. A voice in a different tone suddenly punctuated the conversation: "Who are you, gringo? What are you doing here?" It took me a while to realize that the question must have been directed at me. The person asking the question stepped forward into the firelight, a short, stocky man with a mop of curly hair and a bushy beard of a sort I'd hardly ever seen before on any local man. "He's not a gringo, he's from Britain," responded Juan on my behalf as my brain raced to find a response. "He's a gringo who's spying on us for the CIA," insisted this bearded man. "No, I'm not," I responded and then tried to provide as succinct an account as I could of why I was at the lake. He, however, was drunkenly belligerent, and nothing I could say could convince him otherwise. This frustration made me in turn equally belligerent. "And who are you?" I asked him. "Ask any of these people, they all know me," I continued.

I later discovered that the man had a Mapuche father from the island and a white mother, and had been born, raised, and lived in Santiago. He would return every two or three years to visit his paternal kin here at the lake. Many local people dismissed him as a "terrorist," as he managed to combine a particular brand of Chilean nationalism, international socialism, and what looked like Indigenous activism. Perhaps not unreasonably, US foreign policy in Latin America seemed to be the point at which all of his political analyses began and ended. After a while, I realized that our argument had developed its own symmetrical and self-perpetuating structure: he would accuse me of being an American spy, and I would explain that I was not. This went on back and forth for about fifteen minutes or so, our voices increasing in volume with each iteration. I spoke to Juan in Mapudungun, which made the bearded man even more irate, as he, like many Mapuche people raised in Santiago, couldn't speak it. "You see, that's proof! You've just learned Mapuche to infiltrate our communities! That's what the CIA do!"

Earlier in the day, while the games of *palin* were still going strong, I'd had an almost identical encounter with an almost identical man, also with a Mapuche father and white mother, also raised in Santiago and newly returned to the lake, also with a big bushy beard, and also convinced that I was some kind of CIA operative. There, too, I had tried to explain who I was and what I was doing. My friend Rosita had tried to defend me, but again, speaking Mapudungun with her was interpreted as further evidence of my professional training in international espionage. On that first occasion, I had felt cornered into delivering a rather low blow. The man's maternal surname happened to be the same as that of one of the most spectacularly bloodthirsty of all the Spanish conquistadors, a rather bitter irony for somebody whose identity was centered around being an Indigenous activist. But feeling myself the victim of a great injustice, I was happy to use this against him, only referring to him, loudly and repeatedly, by his maternal surname: not one of my greatest moments, I know, but it seemed to at least temporarily hold him at bay.

In the evening encounter by the fire, it transpired that the man who had accused me earlier that day was the cousin of the man who stood in front of me now, the flames lighting up his angry face, convinced beyond doubt of my malevolent intentions.

I held a *wüño* in my hand, the long, heavy stick used to play the hockey-like game of *palin*, and it seemed to me that the time for words had come to an end. We were throwing them at each other again and again, but these words seemed to get smaller, more impotent, bounce off us and fall flaccidly to the ground only to be picked up and hurled again. I raised the *wüño* and was already visualizing using it to smash this man's squat nose back into his squat face when

Juan stepped in front of me and held my arm. I was corralled out of the area as the bearded man, too, was led away by friends.

I was livid for days. While I complained bitterly, Marta just laughed, saying, "They're all terrorists, what do you expect?" She took particular glee in telling me this because for months now I'd been trying to convince her that Mapuche activists were anything but "terrorists," that rather they were people legitimately defending people like Marta herself against the constant pillaging of their lands by the most voracious neoliberal capitalist machine imaginable. The label "terrorist" was thrown around by the right-wing Chilean media as a way of delegitimizing the Mapuche cause without even addressing the fundamental issues at stake. I should say that the last time I saw Marta, some twenty years later, she had come around to my way of thinking, thanks not to me but to the patient explanations of her children. Yet at that earlier time, many Mapuche people around the lake were very dismissive of Mapuche resistance in other parts of the south; these communities in conflict seemed a very long way away from them, both geographically and socially

Reflecting on this now, after so many years, I wonder why this lie, more than all the other lies I encountered, was the one that hurt me so much, that drove me to the brink of violence? I suppose the answer was the truth that it held within it. US foreign policy has indeed profoundly affected Chile, and to this day Mapuche communities are frequently under all kinds of surveillance, from tapped phones to drones to paid informers. And on some level, even though I knew I was neither American nor a CIA operative trying to destroy Mapuche communities, I was dimly aware that I did indeed occupy a place in the same structure that this global politics had established, a place in which I benefited from a profound and enduring asymmetry bought at other people's cost. This realization was a long time coming, but years later, controversy and accusation would eventually hammer the point home.

*   *   *

The numbingly deep blue skies that appear as permanent fixtures in my memory of the lake were probably fewer and further between in reality. So often, a milky gray haze set in for days on end, accompanied by a persistent drizzle that penetrated everything. But my days on the lake on Eduvino's boat were, I am still sure, always cast in a golden light. Eduvino lived over on the island and was my friend Javiera's brother-in-law, living a literal stone's throw from her parents' house. He was the friend whose brother's death I wrote about in the last chapter. Eduvino was a quiet man, about my age, and Javiera always ridiculed him for being *bien mapuchado*, "too Mapuche" (like Eduardo), in that he wasn't the most fluent of Spanish speakers and, according to her, his ambitions didn't stretch beyond a good potato harvest and the next carton of wine. But there was far more to Eduvino than this.

Eduvino would embrace all of the bounty that the lake had to offer; he gathered swans' eggs from the deep reedbeds, speared carp in the spring, shot coypu along the lake's muddy edges, and on this particular day of infinite blue sky and golden sun, he was accompanying me in our search for *trawa*, a kind of Chilean coot. Technically, the lake was part of a protected nature reserve that seemed to have been created by the Chilean state on the assumption that Indigenous people necessarily "live at one with nature." In practical terms, this meant that hunting of any kind was prohibited in and around the lake. Yet the only notifications of this ban were posted along the highways into and out of the reserve, so most of the people actually living within its confines seemed blissfully unaware of the restrictions and continued to fish and hunt as they had always done. Recently, crackdowns on unlicensed firearms due to the "terrorist threat" posed by Mapuche communities seem to have reduced any hunting that local people do, but the explosion of eucalyptus plantations and chemical fertilizers has taken an even greater toll on local wildlife than hunting and fishing ever did.

Eduvino, however, didn't even need a gun to hunt ducks; he would just throw pebbles at them. He explained this strange and somewhat surprising fact to me as we walked along the road to the southern end of the island, where we were going to borrow his friend's small rowing boat. I'd been wondering why every few paces, he would bend and pick up a pebble from the gravel road and place it in the ubiquitous pink potato sack slung over his shoulder. I'd heard of people hunting with slingshots before, but never just throwing pebbles. I was intrigued, but also somewhat disappointed, having been looking forward to the thrill of blasting away with an antique shotgun.

Eduvino's friend who had the boat wasn't at home, but Eduvino assured me that it would be fine if we just took his boat, which was moored in a small inlet. As we clambered into the small wooden boat and moved away from the shore, Eduvino pointed to the thick reed-beds on either side and told me to keep an eye out for coypu. In fact, during all of my years at the lake and on all my subsequent visits, I have never seen a coypu, either dead or alive, although I was constantly being told that their meat was the most delicious of all.

The small inlet in which the boat had been moored was heavily forested; tall native trees curled over the water from every side. I'd never seen such trees grown so big before—over most of the region they had already been logged and replaced with the ubiquitous eucalyptus. Immense southern beeches created cathedral-like spaces under their green embrace. Eduvino pulled hard on the oars, the tendons in his forearms raised taut against his brown skin, darkened by the endless work of the fields. The boat surged forward with each long stroke, and we'd soon left the inlet behind and headed out into the open water of the lake. The complex topology of the lake's basin—its intricate maze of hills and gullies—made this kind of open perspective rare and somewhat unnerving, as I had had almost no idea of the scale of the lake by which I'd been living for months. Huge flocks of birds that I'd never seen before seemed to cluster in small flocks on different sections of the lake's surface, and eventually Eduvino spotted a pair of coots not far away.

The logic of hunting coots with pebbles is cruel but simple, and I soon realized that you don't actually even need to hit the coot with the pebbles. When alarmed, the coot dives underwater and swims for ten yards or so in the direction it was facing when it submerged. The rowing boat follows the submerged coot in this direction, and as soon as it rises to the surface, the crewperson pelts it with pebbles, forcing it to submerge once more. After its third or fourth dive, the coot is exhausted and just sits forlornly on the surface. A quick whack over the head with Eduvino's oar, and the bedraggled dead bird is placed, like most things in rural Mapuche life, into a salmon-pink potato sack.

Despite the fierce sunshine, the day was not warm, and Eduvino was wearing a thick knitted wool sweater. After his exertions at rowing, however, he was dripping in sweat and had to stand up in the shaky boat to remove the sweater. I couldn't help thinking that he'd expended far more calories in chasing down the poor scrawny coot than its meager meat could possibly replace, but maybe I was missing the point. Over the course of the afternoon, we rowed, or rather Eduvino rowed, frantically from one corner of the lake to the other, lifting entire flocks of ducks from the water's murky surface. I think we'd caught about six or seven of these coots, but once the water had drenched the air from their feathers they seemed to rapidly diminish in size and barely covered the bottom of the sack. Eduvino looked shattered. "Next time we'll bring a gun," he gasped. I took the oars, and using my own idiosyncratic rowing style, did my best to direct us toward home. The sun was setting and the reedbeds came alive with color and light. I steered the boat in an erratic zigzag back to the small inlet, now shrouded in deep shade as the sun faded behind the tall trees. The black-necked swans for which the lake is famous reluctantly parted as the boat slid through the now dark water.

We returned the boat to its mooring and then trudged wearily back along the island's main road until we reached Eduvino's home. A small group of men stood outside drinking, and they were eager to see what riches would emerge from the potato sack. One of these men was known simply as *Chifu*, "Goat." I'm not sure of the exact circumstances of his upbringing, but he'd never been to school and he'd never had an identity card. Not having an identity card is almost inconceivable to most people in Chile. It is the means by which one accesses any kind of education, health care, social security payments, or legal protection; it is often necessary to have for travel on buses and trains, and so on. But Goat had somehow fallen through the cracks, whether by chance or design I'm not quite sure. His life seemed localized, and his lack of any need for an identity card impressed me as an indication of how deeply rooted in this place and this life he was. Goat also happened to be Eduvino's first cousin, a closeness that didn't seem to make Eduvino any less wary of him. It wasn't long before Goat was trying to sneak away with a couple of the birds from the sack; I caught him trying to stuff one in each of his anorak pockets while Eduvino's attention was elsewhere.

Despite the stubbornly egalitarian ethic that pervades almost every aspect of rural Mapuche life, vestiges of hierarchy do occasionally become visible, harking back to those days when a nascent class division had seemed to take root in Mapuche society. At the top were the *toki* warlords, the *ñidol lonko* overchiefs, and the *lonko* headmen, all part of the *ulmen*, the upper parts of society. At the bottom, meanwhile, were the *kona*, the men-at-arms, the peasants. I could never quite get my head around how such a militantly egalitarian society could have so easily morphed into a hierarchical one, and I still can't. Some historians have suggested that this latent hierarchical framework was simply a wartime exigency; that as soon as conflict passed, the egalitarian norm returned. But what became clear to me is that in many rural areas there is still what one might call a Mapuche underclass, usually made up of single, often landless men, who are beholden to others, through various kinds of patronage, for their survival. It was from these men —seemingly already with one foot beyond the bounds of propriety—that clowns were most often recruited. This was the life that Goat led, wandering from homestead to homestead, receiving food and a place to sleep in exchange for agricultural labor. It was usually extended kin he stayed with, aunts or uncles or distant cousins, rarely beyond the confines of the island. He would stay in each place for a couple of months before some row or other forced him to move on. Now he had come full circle and was back staying at Eduvino's after a few years in other parts of the island.

Like Goat, his friend Merengue, too, was landless and homeless. I knew him as Sebastián's nephew, and he could occasionally be found living with Sebastián, but he rarely lasted more than a couple of days there before some bitter argument saw him on his way once more. As we stood around that evening after our duck-hunting trip, while Eduvino went to relieve himself behind the barn, I noticed Merengue, clearly inspired by Goat's attempt, sneaking another two coots out of the sack. I would have remonstrated with him but for the fact that I really didn't want to have to eat the bedraggled balls of black feathers myself. Eduvino, however, was not so forgiving. When he realized what had happened—that there were only two coots left at the bottom of the sack—he demanded that the stolen coots be returned. He had no hesitation in correctly identifying the culprits. Reluctantly, Goat and Merengue returned the limp birds to the sack, now in an even more ragged state than before. Eventually, Eduvino's wife Ignacia called us into the house, but when Eduvino invited Goat and Merengue to follow us in as well, she looked exasperated. They owed her money, but would continue to demand more wine on credit.

People like Goat and Merengue, who make up this hidden under-class, never quite correspond to how Mapuche society sees itself: neither the Mapuche society of the older generation, which still strives for respect in the eyes of *winka*, nor, even less so, that of the younger generation, rooted in the urban experience and looking to rural areas for clear frameworks of Indigenous organization and authority, Mapuche social and cultural institutions that can go toe-to-toe with their Chilean counterparts in the quest for autonomy and recognition. But these people, whose experience is absent from almost all public and academic discourse about Mapuche society, are nevertheless Mapuche in a deeply profound sense, not solely because they speak the Mapuche language and bear Mapuche surnames but because they are truly of the land: they know it and, ironically, their poverty leads them to know it better than most, as they seek out the swans' nests, the spawning fish, the crayfish at the lake's edge, and the coots hidden at the bottom of the sack.

* * *

The beauty, silence, and mystery of the native woodland stand in stark contrast to the vast plantations of eucalyptus and pine that dominate so much of southern Chile and that, planted on stolen Mapuche land as they are, have become the cause of so much suffering. While most of these plantations are on a truly industrial scale, run by predominantly Scandinavian forestry operations, Mapuche people themselves have been attempting to cash in on the timber boom in a low-key way. Many homesteads have small stands of eucalyptus planted on any ground that is too steep to plow. Alternatively, they use lines of eucalyptus to demarcate boundaries. There are also some small plantations of pine, what people call *cipre*, but the exhilarating speed at which eucalyptus grows, and the occasionally high prices it demands, have ensured its ubiquity. Yet everybody knows the cost that it comes at: for eucalyptus is a thirsty tree, sucking all the moisture from the land. A large plantation can dry out the ground for miles around, leaving it vulnerable to erosion and degradation in the harsh southern wind. Mapuche communities neighboring the large-scale plantations further to the north and to the south have found agriculture increasingly untenable, the streams upon which they have depended for generations drying up to nothing. People are aware of these ecological consequences, but as is so often the case, their poverty means that they have little choice but to exploit every last square yard of their land, and eucalyptus allows them to do just that.

Yet despite everything, it's hard to deny that they are beautiful trees: long, straight trunks reaching ever skywards, mottled beige-and-gray bark falling away in strips, elegant gray-green leaves, and such a pungent smell that the air itself seems stripped back to a primordial cleanliness. Their leaves have now become an established part of traditional Mapuche medicine, *lawen*, for the treatment of coughs and colds, boiled into a steam bath or tea.

One fog-enshrouded morning, Sebastián called for me at the homestead. He had come to offer me the "opportunity" to observe him felling trees, by which he meant that he was a man down and needed some help. Sebastián was my friend from over on the island and had been born and raised in the place where he still lived, *Chalwatuwe*, "the place of fish." He had lost an eye to a glass bottle in a fight at a *ngillatun* ritual several years previously, which gave him something of a permanently bemused look. Or maybe he was just permanently bemused. I loved spending time with him, but I was aware that many feared him, apparently for a tyrannical side that he had but from which my status as a foreigner and the color of my skin protected me. I saw Sebastián again last year, but he'd become old, unwell, and tired. "*Tripawelay*," "he no longer goes out," they said of him, the functional end of a Mapuche man's life. I realize now that even when I'd known him best, he was perhaps beyond his prime. He could still hold a room with his renditions of Mexican country classics, but people didn't listen the way they once had. Sebastián had had a series of daughters and no sons, so, saddened to be without an heir, he'd adopted the son of a neighbor. Only a year after this adoption, his wife Constanza became pregnant with twins, two boys, leaving Sebastián with a surfeit of sons. It was one of these sons, Pitu, who accompanied him on the day he took me along to cut down trees.

Using remittances sent by his children who were away working in Santiago, Sebastián had invested in a Husqvarna chainsaw. This chainsaw, I had to concede, was a thing of beauty, oozing power and danger in equal measure, an impression that increased tenfold when the terrifying sound of its motor ripped into the silence. Sebastián earned a little bit of money logging eucalyptus in the communities around the lake, charging a percentage of the profit from the sale of the timber. The trees were felled, measured, and cut off into meter-long lengths, which were then stacked together to form "metroruma" square meters of wood, the unit in which eucalyptus is bought and sold. That day, the three of us left the homestead and headed off deeper into the isthmus between the lake and the ocean. We were to log a stand of eucalyptus belonging to a Pentecostal family not far from the sea cliffs, so given their teetotalism, the chances of us receiving anything to drink, or even any hospitality at all, seemed remote. Perhaps this was why Sebastián seemed in an even brusquer mood than usual; he wouldn't even let me carry the chainsaw, which we all agreed was the prestige task.

From a distance, the communities of the central isthmus seem topologically flat, but when you enter them you realize that they are in fact cut through by steep-sided gullies, usually filled with native plants such as the beautiful bell-shaped *copihue*, or *ñalka*, a kind of giant rhubarb tasting a bit like celery. It was along the slopes of one of these gullies that the stand of eucalyptus we were to cut stood. There was nobody else about, and both Pitu and I worried that we might cut down the wrong trees. Sebastián, however, seemed confident.

The steep slope was covered in the fallen leaves of the trees, weathered from pale gray to a milky beige. Underfoot, they slipped and rolled, snowballing down the slope toward the creek. I slipped once or twice as we made our way down toward where we would start logging, making me think that perhaps it wasn't such a bad thing after all that I wasn't carrying the chainsaw. As we got to our destination, Sebastián transitioned into didactic mode and explained that two ropes would be tied to the tree to be felled, with Pitu holding the end of one and me the end of the other. Once the tree started to fall, Pitu and I were to guide its crashing descent away from the other trees and toward the clear ground, where it was to be further divided. The first tree that we were going to take down was one of the biggest in the stand, and as I realized just how tall it was, I started to become a little apprehensive. "Isn't this a bit dangerous?" I asked Sebastián. "Only if it lands on you," was his reassuring response. "Look, if it starts to fall toward you, run up the slope, and Pitu will pull it back toward him. It'll be fine." I looked at Pitu, who at that moment seemed both distracted and far too small to pull a falling giant eucalyptus away from my direction. But as has so often been the case in my life, I couldn't see a face-saving way out, and I weakly assented.

The whine of the chainsaw leapt up in pitch as its whirring teeth bit into the trunk, and the pungent smell of eucalyptus filled the air. Sebastián first cut a small notch in the downhill-facing side of the trunk, a notch that would ideally determine the direction in which the tree fell. He then shuffled around, through the thick leaves on the gully floor, to the other side of the trunk and commenced on the bigger notch, the one that would bring the tree down. Various groans emerged from the trunk, until a sharp crack signaled the beginning of its fall. Sebastián scrambled quickly out of the way, as trees can often slip back off their stumps while falling, sometimes crushing the feet or legs of a logger not fast enough to spring out of the way. Trees always seem to start falling in slow motion, and this one toppled slowly in the direction Sebastián had intended. But halfway through its decline, the tree seemed to pause—and then some knot, hidden deep inside its trunk, caused it to twist around and start falling directly toward me. I could see the rope in Pitu's hands tauten, and to his credit, he didn't let go. He did, however, find it completely impossible to maintain his footing in the fallen silver foliage, and the thought flashed through my mind that my last sight on this earth would be the rather incongruous one of a man water-skiing on leaves. I dropped the rope and ran, or at least tried to run, up the hill, away from the falling tree. Yet every other step I took seemed to slip from underneath me as layers of the papery leaves slid across each other under my feet. A couple of seconds later, the tree crashed down around me, a gray-green haze of mentholated chaos.

I opened my eyes, awaiting searing pain from some catastrophic injury, but aside from a few sharp scratches, I was unharmed. It appeared that I'd been swatted off my feet by the tree's feathery upper reaches, rather than being hit by the heavy trunk or any of the major branches. As I sat up, my head poked through the dense foliage and I saw Pitu's face, deathly pallid. I imagine I looked much the same. Sebastián, however, just burst out laughing, muttering away about "squashing gringos." From then on, I stayed away from the felling of the trees and worked quietly and diligently to place the sections of trunk into neat stacks, for sale to the timber buyers who moved sporadically through the area, looking for small profits in the niches and gullies that the industrial plantations had left behind. When the day was done, there was no wine, no cider, and no food; we just trudged back home. Sebastián still wouldn't let me hold the chainsaw.

*   *   *

Later that month, I headed to the island to meet Sebastián once more, this time in the hope of conducting a long-promised and oft-postponed interview on how his particular community had come into being, a hundred years previously, in the wake of war and displacement. I'd barely set foot through the outer gate of Sebastián's homestead, onto the patio, when somebody behind me called my name. It was Fernando, a large and brutal man whom many people feared, but who seemed to hold me in high regard. Maybe it was just my status as a white foreigner, a reputed bearer of great power and wealth, but I like to think it was because I was one of relatively few people who were prepared to spend time with him and hear what he had to say. Rumors buzzed around him like flies around a cow's eyes: that he'd beaten one wife to death, and that another had barely escaped

with her life. That he knew things—that he was not exactly a practic-
ing witch but somebody who understood the perverse mechanics of
how such things worked. It was this aura of barely restrained brutal-
ity, combined with his ample frame, that earned him the nickname
Huacho—a large pig fenced in and overfed to provide an extra layer
of fat. Only the brave, of course, would have dared utter this name
in his presence. I always called him Don Fernando, a formality that
seemed to both please and surprise him. I remember us once sitting
together at a bus stop by the main road around the lake, soaking in
the white light of the winter sun, while he told me one of the "things"
he knew: that in a certain gully, in a certain community, two trees
grew side by side. These trees had become so intertwined that their
trunks had eventually become one. Through the incantation of a few
choice words over this knotted pair, one could ensure the possession
of one's beloved. He was preparing to tell me what these words were
when the bus arrived, and my romantic future was left to be deter-
mined by other means.

This morning at Sebastián's, however, Fernando was not his usual
relaxed self. He didn't give me his customary welcoming bear hug,
squeezing me to his broad belly and rubbing his bright white bristles and mustache against my face. No, this morning Fernando had a
problem. The threshing machine had arrived to process his harvest,
but he didn't have enough help to load the cut wheat into one end of
the machine or to sew the grain sacks shut at the other. Most Mapuche men can happily rely on their neighbors and relatives to help
them in this kind of collective task, through the reciprocal shared
labor of a *mingako* work party. Fernando, however, was barely on
speaking terms with anybody, hence his pleas for my assistance that
morning. It dawned on me then, as I prepared to exchange a day of
hard labor for no money and little chance of any food or drink, that
the exploitation involved in the anthropological enterprise wasn't
always a one-way street. Maybe that's unfair, though: I can't deny that
there's something about the wheat harvest that always drew me in. I

don't know if it was the warmth of summer, the smell of hay, or the intensity of the work, but it always seemed infinitely more interesting than the unyielding, muddy, monotonous slog of harvesting potatoes in the winter. Perhaps it was down to reading too much Thomas Hardy in school—the harvest as a bucolic idyll behind which tragedy always lurked—for whatever reason, I promised Fernando that I'd meet him at his field within the hour.

By the time I'd finished listening to Fernando's plea and crossing the patio to Sebastián's door, Sebastián was already leaning out of it, laughing hysterically. I knew what he'd say and I wasn't disappointed. "Why on earth are you going to help that fat bastard? You'll see, he won't give you anything. No food, no drink, and no money," he said. "It'll be good for my research," I replied somewhat sheepishly. "So why don't you just go and watch? You're not going to see anything buried in a haystack." Through his laughter, Sebastián reached for his cap and jacket and made for the door. "Where are you going?" I asked. "Fernando's. I'm coming too." "You're coming to help as well?" "Help! Are you fucking kidding me? I'm going for the wine!" Sebastián was still laughing when we reached Fernando's field, half an hour later. The harvested field lay between the main road and his house, set back a couple of hundred yards or so from the road. Just the sharp stubble remained; the sheaves of wheat had already been gathered in and brought to the large patio in front of the small house. It was a warm day, the southern sun shone fiercely, and I could already feel my pale skin burning. The large red thresher's engine was pumping out thick black fumes of smoke, but there was nobody to do the work of cutting the binding of the sheaves and spreading out the cut wheat onto the conveyor belt of the thresher. The operator of the machine, who was also its owner, looked exasperated and on the verge of losing it altogether. He was a Mapuche man from further south, from the richer, "more organized" communities beyond Inalafken where mechanized agriculture was already the norm for everybody due to flatter, more profitable land. He was scowling at a small huddle of

men who were already fairly wasted. I recognized these men; they
were the usual suspects, men who turned up to drink rather than to
work, although sometimes when the mood took them they would
flare up into a sudden burst of energy and fling themselves at the task
at hand. Maybe Fernando had gambled on this latter outcome.

Fernando himself was nowhere to be seen when we arrived. He'd
apparently gone off to get supplies a while earlier and hadn't returned
yet. The operator looked pleadingly at me and Sebastián, but Sebastián
just laughed and joined the small group of drinkers. I scrambled my
way to the top of the huge pyramid of sheaves, towering twenty or so
feet above the thresher. I would throw the tightly bundled sheaves
down to somebody next to the conveyor belt feeding the machine.
The operator himself would tie the sacks filling up with the precious
grain. It was normally a six-person job; two men throwing sheaves
down, two loading the belt, and two women sewing shut the grain
sacks. It could just about be done with three, but there were unfortunately only two of us willing to work, myself and the operator. Just
as I was about to give up and descend from the giant stack, a forlorn,
grubby child of around ten or eleven emerged from Fernando's house
and quietly took up position next to the conveyor belt. The operator
and I looked at one another; the child was clearly too small to catch
heavy bundles being hurled from a great height while standing next
to the gaping intestines of a ferocious piece of agricultural machinery.
Nobody even seemed to know exactly who the child was, as all of Fernando's children had bolted to the city or to the vineyards of the north
as soon as they were old enough to get away. The consensus was that
this was some errant grandchild, sent to his ostracized grandfather as
a particularly draconian punishment. I insisted on swapping places
with the kid, figuring that he was at less risk up on the stack than next
to the thresher. He certainly managed to scramble up it quicker than
I had done.

The operator clicked the thresher into gear, and like colic moving
through a sheep, the sounds inside the machine shifted in location and

pitch. The belt started moving and the threshing began. Each sheaf of wheat had been tied together into a barrel-like shape—roughly the girth of a man—with a specific kind of reed, the name of which I've now forgotten. It was incredibly durable and strong, but if given a sharp tug, it would snap. The idea was to drop the sheaf toward the belt and just as it was about to land, to yank your hand back suddenly, breaking the reed and spilling the wheat out onto the conveyor belt in neat alignment, but the procedure was far from foolproof. Frequently the reed would fail to snap, and then my forearm felt like it was about to be wrenched out at the elbow. At other times, the sheaf would spring back and hit me in the face. The worst thing was when the reed snapped before being lifted up; then I had to scramble around to scrape the individual stalks up from the dirt. The one constant in all of this was the sharp sides of the reed cutting into my hand with each tug, so that within a quarter of an hour my hand was dripping with blood.

The situation deteriorated when the still-unnamed boy at the top of the haystack realized that by hurling down the sheaves slightly prematurely, he could knock me off my feet. The first time he did it, I thought it was quite funny. The second time less so. The novelty of being hit in the head by a thirty-kilo bundle of spiky wheat wore off pretty quickly. My initial concerns about him being mangled by agricultural machinery rapidly diminished, so I insisted on swapping roles again, sending him down to the thresher while I went up the stack. "What the hell are you doing?" a voice shouted from below. "You can't let a child work the belt." It was Sebastián, a by now well-lubricated Sebastián. "I'm not coming down," I yelled back. "If you don't want him to work it, you can work it yourself."

As I have often found it to be the case with men of a certain age, a little wine made Sebastián more rather than less amenable to work; I have always been the opposite way, and could never quite understand it. But being on top of the stack was far more enjoyable; I really did feel like the king of the castle surveying my domain. Tossing the huge sheaves down was certainly fun, and I even embraced the boy's trick of a slightly premature release, thus knocking Sebastián off his feet with the heavy sheaves of wheat. Given that Sebastián was in his late sixties, walked with a cane, and only had one eye, this might have been a little insensitive on my part, but the satisfaction was immense.

By now it was lunchtime, and usually workers would be expecting the *ngen kudaw*—"the master of work" for whom we were laboring—to call us in for lunch. But Fernando was still nowhere to be seen. And anyway, there would be no lunch, as there was nobody to cook it on his behalf. He no longer had a wife and would certainly not deign to cook himself even if he were able. It was not unreasonable, however, for us to expect him to at least provide us with a little cider to see us through the heat of the day, and maybe a carton of wine or two to unwind when night came. Just then, we heard a loud whoop from the top of the field. It was Fernando, with another three or four men in tow, and from the further whoops and the zigzag path they cut through the stubble, it was fairly clear that they at least had been drinking. "I've brought help," said Fernando, in a tone that seemed to expect some degree of gratitude. He held two big plastic bags, one in each hand, and I hoped that they contained food, or perhaps some kind of soft drink. As he set them down, though, it became clear that they held nothing other than cartons of lukewarm white wine.

And yet, despite the absence of lunch, the new arrivals did successfully lift the mood. These kinds of tasks were often dependent on a kind of frenetic collective momentum; when people really threw themselves into the task, others followed. The fact that the new arrivals were all half-cut meant that they embraced the work with an impressive fervor. Fernando's neighbor Martín joined me at the top of the haystack and we created a little chain; he'd throw the sheaves from the far side of the stack to me, and I would then throw them down to the guy by the conveyor belt. Martín was better known as *Kumaw*, "Intestinal Worm," because he had been infested with these worms throughout his childhood and because his resultant protruding belly endured into his adult years. We worked happily and diligently through the afternoon, and as we worked, the stack on which we stood steadily diminished. Eventually, we reached ground level, and the last few stalks of wheat were run through the thresher. The job was done, and as far as I could tell, Fernando hadn't lifted a finger all day long.

The early evening light of late summer is for me the most perfect and most evocative of all light. Like a forgotten scent, it can only take us back to better days, days of comfort, warmth, and promise. We sat on an old log, taking in this peach-orange light, as people shared out wine from the cartons that Fernando had given them. There seemed to be some kind of negative correlation between work carried out and wine received, but then I realized that Fernando was simply reciprocating gifts of wine he himself had received earlier in the day. These were poor people, and the wine they drank was not Chile's finest. Nevertheless, with a body slowly piecing itself back together after an intense day of work, the happy atmosphere following the completion of the harvest, and the sweet melancholy of that summer light, it tasted good, full, and strong in my mouth. Because wine is always shared out and drunk from a single circulating glass in that context, individuals can't really set the pace of the drinking; it emerges as a cumulative collective decision. And I could feel it filling my empty stomach, filling my tired head, filling my desire. We drank until there was no more, and then headed off to remedy this lack. Fernando fell asleep in the *chacra*, the harvested field, and Sebastián, I, and a couple of other men headed back up to Sebastián's house in Chalwatuwe as the first stars of the night registered in the great southern sky.

Back at Sebastián's, people were buying and swapping wine at a speedy pace. Several glasses were in circulation at once and would occasionally overtake one another, depending on the speed of the drinker. Although this way of drinking can be somewhat coercive, it also offers the possibility of subterfuge: you can simply fake it, mimicking a sip but swallowing nothing. This was the tactic I tried to resort to in most such situations, but it's only ever a temporary measure.

Sooner or later, the drink grabs you and won't put you down. When the room started to swim around me, I swayed and staggered from the kitchen, not saying good-bye to anyone, as people avoid shaking hands after dark so as to avoid inadvertently passing on the Devil or some parasitic demon. The summer night was perfect, the stars shone brighter than I'd ever seen, there was a warm breeze against my skin. I knew I was beyond drunk, but I knew, too, that the world was with me. Lurching forward, I made my way across the patio, avoiding the sleeping dogs, to Sebastián's outside hay loft, filled with fresh hay the previous day when the thresher had done its rounds.

I clawed my way up the rough ladder and burrowed my way into the elevated loft. Curled up, I gently rocked myself back and forth, creating a nest in the hay, letting the world mold itself to my form. I thought for an instant of those strange divots in the sides of Scottish mountains, worn away over years by sheep curling themselves into the earth against the wind. Tonight there was little wind; just the sky, a deepest and darkest blue, and the southern stars shining brightly. I knew I would pay the price in the morning, but for now I felt at peace with the world flowing through me. There is something about curling into sleep in an outdoor corner that fills me with calm. Perhaps it's looking back to the safety and warmth of the womb, but maybe it's looking forward to the hour of our death, a hope for a quiet return, for silence, for stillness.

*   *   *

In the spring, the risen winter waters of the lake start to recede. They pull back from the lake's outermost margins and make accessible what by summertime has dried out into flower-filled meadows. In the spring, however, these meadows are still submerged in about a foot of brackish water. It is in these grassy shallows that carp come to spawn in great numbers. While fishermen from the small port on the other side of the lake fish for carp with nets, on this western

side of the lake people fish for them with tridents, *wayki* in Mapudungun. These tridents consist of a three-pronged head, with each
prong bearing a vicious barb. The head is attached to a long pole, the
length of which at first seems excessive because it makes the trident
feel heavy, unwieldy, and unbalanced. The idea is simply to wade
stealthily through the water, spearing the lascivious and distracted
carp as you go along and placing them into an old potato sack slung
over your shoulder. These are fairly sizable, substantial fish, maybe a
couple of kilos each on average.

Fishing for carp sounded like my idea of a good time and when
Mateo bounded into the kitchen one October morning to tell us
that the carp were spawning at the lake's edge just below the house,
I leapt into action. Juan had an old trident head, but the once-long
pole to which it was still attached had broken off into a short rot-
ten stump. Nevertheless, he seemed confident that we could craft a
new shaft easily enough. We rose from the kitchen table and headed
straight out to a small stand of eucalyptus saplings on a south-facing
slope. Juan quickly identified one of the correct length and girth, and
felled it with a single swing of his axe. A few more delicate blows
and he had trimmed and stripped the bark. He trimmed one end
down, inserted it into the trident head, and secured it with an old nail
wrenched from a nearby fencepost. I was still somewhat unclear as
to why the shaft was so long, but Juan explained to me that the extra
length would allow me to throw the trident further and straighter if
the carp were gathering out of reach.

Then, as I leaned the newly restored trident up against the fence
and made my way back to the house to get my Wellington boots, Juan
exclaimed, "You can't wear boots! The water will just pour in over the
top. You've got to just wear shorts and go barefoot." Given that the
southern spring had only recently appeared, and that a frost still lay
heavy on the ground, the thought of slipping into shorts and padding
barefoot through a lake gave me pause. I didn't even know if I had
any shorts. But a quick rummage underneath my bed produced a

slightly moldy pair of swimming trunks, which I slipped into before heading out the door.

Having made my way down to the edge of the lake, I could see that the carp were indeed abundant and active. Even from a hundred yards away, their thick bodies were visibly boiling the water. So I stepped out of my boots and crept over the last few yards of soft grass to the water's edge. The ground here was soft and spongy, the grass having been closely cropped by animals eager to pasture after winter's deprivations. It took me a couple of delicate steps into the water to realize just how cold it was. A numb ache grew from within the center of each of my feet and worked its way out to my toes and up into my ankles. As I stepped further in, the water reached my calves and then my knees, and my breath changed to short, sharp sucks of air as the pain reached my head. I managed to tell myself that the agony would subside, but it was more a case of new waves of pain superseding the old, a constant renewal of distraction that made it just about bearable. The water stayed shallow for a good ten yards, and I was able to get fairly close to where the carp were congealing.

The fact that the carp were so heaped together, turning and rolling their green-gold bellies to the white-gold sun, did not, as I had initially assumed, work to my advantage. It was hard to find a single fish to aim at, so I just hurled the trident into the writhing mass. Nothing. The fish paused, and then resumed their activities as if nothing had happened. It wasn't quite clear what, exactly, they were doing, and I realized that the technicalities of how fish go about spawning was something about which I was completely ignorant. One thing was clear, however: their urge to reproduce had stripped them all of their usual cautiousness. Like clowns, the staid routines of their lives had been overcome by desire. They swam around my legs, and for a brief moment, I felt paralyzing fear: their thick, scaly bodies would overwhelm me if they worked collectively. Fragmented memories of piranha movies I'd seen as a child seeped into my mind. But recovering the trident stuck into the submerged grass, I tried to collect my thoughts and reconsider my strategy.

This time, I decided it would be best to focus on a single fish, one of the ones skirting the edge of the main bulk of the shoal. And rather than throw the trident, I would simply strike without releasing, hopefully exerting a bit more control and accuracy that way. A dark shape veered away from the rest and moved toward me; when it veered again, revealing its broad side, I thrust with the trident. I couldn't possibly have missed, I was sure. The fish had been right by my feet. I reached down, assuming that the trident had gone through the fish, pinning it to the lake bottom, but there was nothing there. I was baffled; how could I have missed? I repeated the thrust in slow motion and noticed the sudden shift of angle the trident made as it pierced the water's surface. I vaguely remembered having studied this effect—the refraction of light through water—years earlier at school. Yet I still wasn't quite sure how to adjust accordingly: should I aim above or below where I saw the fish to be? A few more failed thrusts and I began to think that ignorance of physics was only one element of the problem—maybe I just couldn't hit the target. Two cows stood behind me on the bank, one red, one black, both watching me intently.

I was starting to get very cold, and despite the seasonal tug upon their reproductive organs, the carp were beginning to disperse in the wake of my thrashing, thrusting, and plunging. How could something so simple, with fish so large and abundant, be so difficult? My toes appeared to have gone through several color changes since entering the water: first red, then purple, now a kind of insipid yellow, like tobacco-stained fingers. This, combined with a complete lack of sensation in my extremities, led me to turn toward the bank and home. I was bitterly disappointed, and in my frustration I hurled my trident ten yards away, toward where the carp were now amassing once more. But as I walked away, I remembered that the trident actually belonged to Juan, and so just abandoning it to the lake in fury was not really an option. And as I came close to retrieve it, I noticed a large carp that seemed to be hovering around it, in maybe only half a foot of water. It appeared that the trident was pinning the carp to the lake floor through the very end of its lip, the most delicate of margins. It struck me that so delicate was the trident's hold on the fish that any great flapping could see it break free. It also struck me that this was a big fish and that simultaneously lifting it out with one hand while removing a heavy trident with the other, all in icy cold water, was not going to be easy.

I slipped my hand gently under the carp's belly, but it seemed to be covered in some kind of slime that I didn't want to think about too deeply. I felt that the potato sack had a sufficiently textured quality, so I looped it over my hand like some kind of overgrown pink mitten. Lifting trident and fish at the same time, I managed to extract them both and stagger to the shore. The carp flapped on the grass beside me, its large mouth, thick head, and green-and-gold body heaving in and out, until a quick whack over the head with a nearby stick brought it to its end. I felt triumphant as I threaded a green reed through its gills and out of its mouth so that I could carry it the way I'd seen the old men do. I headed back home with my fish, and as I crossed the patio toward the house, Marta stuck her head out of the door: "Is that all? Just one? People usually get ten or twenty!" This was soon followed by her youngest son, Camilo, asking, "Did you actually catch that yourself? Are you sure you didn't just buy it off someone?" I was starting to feel somewhat deflated.

Carp are not gutted in the usual manner, by making a delicate incision in the belly, extracting the guts, and leaving the rest of the fish intact. Instead, they are simply cleaved in half lengthwise, from head to tail. Marta did this with a small hatchet, over the stump we usually used to chop wood. The butterflied fish is then attached to the outside of the doorframe, with a nail hammered through its head, and left to dry out for at least a day. Marta explained that carp were very "wet" fish, and that's why they needed to dry out before cooking.

By now the frost of the morning had gone, and the afternoon was a fairly warm one for spring. A westerly wind from the ocean helped dry out the fish to the desired degree. Whereas smaller fish are usually battered and fried, carp are always smeared in the usual *aliño*, a kind of ubiquitous spice blend, and then roasted in a wood-fired oven. Having grown up in Britain, where carp are for the most part held in complete culinary disregard, I didn't have very high expectations, but it was delicious, the moist and deeply savory flesh clinging to large bones. The ribs were so substantial that it almost felt like eating good southern barbecue.

And I have to admit that my enjoyment was increased even more by another thing that had happened earlier that day. In the afternoon, when the carp had once again amassed by the lake's shore, Mateo and his brother Joaquín had pieced the trident back together and, with great confidence, told me that they'd show me how it was really done—that anything less than ten fish was a dismal failure. They returned a couple of hours later with nothing at all.

*   *   *

The last time I saw Challa was in the orchard behind his mother's house. White apple blossoms stuck to his black hair, and tears cut white streaks through the dirt on his face. A blue nylon rope bit taut around his neck and his feet brushed the muddy ground as they swung. A crowd of people slowly gathered and stared. Luis turned away, muttering, "This is what becomes of clowns." For behind the hilarity, joy, and chaos of their ritual actions, the lot of the clown is not a happy one. Within each clown lies his inevitable downfall: Jerónimo, murdered; Challa, taking his own life; Goat, homeless; Motrilu, imprisoned. Abject poverty, illness, alcoholism, and depression are his constant companions and an untimely death his usual fate.

Challa is the Mapuche word for a kind of clay jug, an appropriate nickname for Challa, whose ears protruded at perfect right angles from his head. He was about my age, although deep laugh lines around his eyes always made him seem somewhat older. He had always seemed to me to be surrounded by laughter. He was the second son of his father's second wife. Like many *lonko* headmen, Challa's father had married his first wife's sister as a way of bringing her within the kinship fold and adding to the productive capacity of their household.

I don't remember when I first met Challa; he lived in the neighboring community and was thus always moving in the same circles, at football matches, at work parties, and so on. But the first occasion when I really got to know him was sitting in Motrilu's mother Lucia's kitchen, trying to haggle over the price of a handspun, handwoven, undyed *makuiñ* poncho she had made. I say haggle, but I just gave her what she asked, having witnessed at first hand the countless hours that go into each *makuiñ*. I was trying to ask her a bit about the process, about why some *makuiñ* are so elaborately decorated yet others left as plain as can be, but given her lack of Spanish and my pitiful Mapudungun, I wasn't really getting much further than the term "sheep's wool," *kal ufisha*. She smiled at me with a look of resignation, and I smiled back, equally resigned. She fried me an egg as a small compensation for our communicative failure. At this moment, with the cool dark of evening starting to fall, Challa arrived with Motrilu, Babyface, and a carton of red wine.

Challa seemed at that moment a person entirely open, transparent; without reserve, guardedness, or hesitation. As always, laughter surrounded him. We sat at the small wooden table and more fried eggs arrived as Babyface's perennially acerbic tongue heaped provocation upon us all: Motrilu was scared of women, I was making millions from selling Mapuche secrets, and Challa was nothing but the second son of a second wife. Motrilu grimaced, I bristled with indignation, and Challa just laughed, a warm and fluid chuckle bubbling like the small brook running past outside the window. Each time he served wine from the carton, we all had to shuffle off the bench to enable him to serve Lucia, who sat quietly tending the wood stove as the Spanish words fluttered meaninglessly around her. He showed Lucia a respect verging on the reverential, something that I often saw him repeat with other elderly women in other homesteads, as if every woman were his own mother.

Like Jerónimo, whom years later Motrilu would kill, Challa was a clown, both in the everyday sense of somebody who loved to make others laugh and as somebody who carried out the duties of a ritual clown. He relished charging up and down the lines of ritual dancers on his little wooden hobbyhorse, straw falling out of his overstuffed costume as he berated the dancers for their lack of vigor. And afterward, he enjoyed the clown's prerogative of snatching the food off people's plates, the wine from their glasses, the women from their tables. It was laughter that united his ritual and secular life but also, perhaps, the lack of boundaries. When Challa loved, it was uncontrolled, spilling over, not recognizing the cautious and measured ways through which such things are done.

In Mapudungun, suicide is always phrased as *kisu langumuwi*, "alone, he killed himself"—as though the being alone were the pivotal factor: being shorn of the relationships that would otherwise sustain you and pull you through. The rate of suicide among young Mapuche men is, like that of many Indigenous peoples elsewhere in the Americas, astronomically high. They always die by hanging, always having in the final instance felt themselves to be truly alone. People told me that when a young man decides to kill himself, the Devil himself takes pity upon him and lets him die the second he places the noose around his neck, to diminish his suffering. I was never quite sure what to make of this, but the idea lodged in my mind like an errant splinter, refusing to resolve itself into logic no matter how hard and frequently I worried at it.

Why Challa died, nobody was quite sure. Some people claimed it was because of a woman, and others that he was killed by the Devil himself. Eventually, the prevailing explanation combined these two strands: he had been rejected by a woman, and this rejection had placed him in such an emotionally vulnerable state that the Devil had swooped in and snatched at the opportunity to lead him to suicide. It had just been a fleeting moment, the kind of romantic setback all young people face and are usually quick to forget about. But for Challa, the sense of proportion had been lost; it was the end of his world. I'd never seen a hanged man before, but what I remember is neither shock nor horror, just sadness. My own sadness at his passing, and the sadness to which the trails of tears down his cheeks bore witness.

The next day I went to visit his father, to give him some money. The costs of a funeral can be crippling for rural Mapuche families, as they have the double expense of the costs of a Chilean funeral, including undertakers, an expensive coffin, and transport to and from the morgue in the port, as well as those of a Mapuche funeral, which means food and drink for hundreds of guests at both the wake and the funeral itself. Challa's father, whom I was accustomed to see laughing, like his son, kept his eyes to the ground and looked up only briefly to acknowledge the envelope of money. His mother cried quietly by the stove in the corner.

*   *   *

I'd already done quite a bit of research talking to older people about traditional Mapuche marriage practices before I finally made my way to Luis. In mainstream Chilean society, a lot of predictably derogatory and racist falsehoods surround the idea of Mapuche marriage: that women are kidnapped against their will, or that brides are purchased with cattle. Needless to say, these ideas are twisted caricatures of what actually happens. As we sat together under the broad beech tree arching over his patio, and his notoriously vicious dog eyed me suspiciously from a distance, Luis explained to me how and why Mapuche marriage actually worked. "When I got married, I stole my wife. That's right, I snuck in and stole her while her parents were sleeping. And when they came to ask for her back, I said 'No. Forget it!' A few weeks later, I gave them a cow and they were okay about it. I didn't have to give them a cow, but I wanted to. I didn't want them to feel bad; I wanted them to know that I respected them." "And what about Juana," I asked, somewhat horrified. "How did she feel about being stolen?" "What do you mean?! It was her idea! She knew that her parents wanted to keep her at home to help around the house, and every year they said to her, 'You can get married next summer,' but each time the next summer came around, they said no. So she forced the issue. We were in love and couldn't wait any longer. She set the date and told me to come and that was that. That was fifty years ago." Luis and Juana acted for each other and for their love for each other, a love that over the years has—through children and grandchildren, through harvests and healthy herds—kept life going in their land.

This kind of individual autonomy, this show of inner strength, might at first sight appear to violate social norms, but in another sense it constitutes a social norm in itself: that one should act with one's own conviction and confidence. To act in this way is to be *newenche*, to be a person of force. Yet this strength of will, this determination, only constitutes one as *newenche* if this force, this strength is directed in accordance with the broader values of Mapuche society: love, care, and respect. This force isn't simply a physical force but rather an inner willpower in which one's physical desires are brought into alignment with the desires of others: if I feel hunger, we *all* eat; if I feel thirst, we *all* drink. To be *newenche* is the preserve of neither the old nor the young but is part of one's commitment to the people around one and the land of which one is a part: the force of will to stick with one's convictions and have the inner strength to do what one believes is right.

Clowns might show force in a superficial, physical sense, but they don't know how to direct it outward, toward the desires of others; they don't understand respect. If they want food, they grab it. If they want sex, they grab it. In doing so, they are not only breaching social rules and social decorum but they are completely missing the point behind those rules and that decorum: that respect is another form of love, a form of love that keeps the endless stream of life flowing. The comic figure of the clown certainly makes people laugh, but it also reminds them of what life would look like it if weren't founded upon the love and respect of others, if we all just weakly assented to the immediate self-satisfaction of our own desires: a world of clowns and chaos.

i i i

usurper

Who is the usurper? The usurper is the one who seeks to own, who turns all the things of this world into property, their property. Like the clown they fail to see love, and like the witch they destroy love. The continuous beauty of the world, its flux and its flow, is contained, caged within boundaries, and claimed by the usurper to the exclusion of others.

Mapuche people call the usurper *winka* and their language *winkadungun*. Nobody is quite sure where the word came from. Some say it comes from *we inka*, "the new Inka," those people from far to the north who also sought to own and control. Others say it's from the verb *winkan*, "to usurp," but nobody knows which came first, the usurper or the usurpation.

Perhaps it started with the white missionaries turning Mapuche "souls" into their property, before the usurper then moved on to their land, their bodies, their selves. And through this process many Mapuche, too, have become white people, *awinkado*, as they say, turning their lands and lives into things to be sold, accepting that different vision of the world and all it entails.

*   *   *

The first time I met Kod-Kod, he threatened to kill me. Juan, his youngest son Camilo, and I had loaded up the oxcart with sacks of apples that we had gathered the previous day. We'd then made the short but difficult journey across to the island, as the oxen slipped and skidded on the muddy slopes either side of the ford across the lake. There were other people already at Kod-Kod's, and they were all there for the same reason as us: pressing apples. Cider, *chicha* as it is known in Spanish, or *manshana pülko*, "apple wine," in Mapudungun, is a big thing in southern Chile. From late summer until the end of autumn, people gather apples and take them to be pressed at the three or four places around the lake with a cider press, paying either a small amount of cash or a percentage of the produce. The sweet fresh juice is then stored in any available containers and left to ferment; Juan had invested in two huge 200-liter plastic barrels; others simply used anything to hand, from old buckets to plastic diesel containers, and it wasn't unusual for the cider to bear a genealogical trace of the former contents of its receptacle, drinkers wearing a slight grimace at the underlying chemical tang.

Some of the juice is drunk straight away, the nonalcoholic *chicha dulce*. Most of it, however, is allowed to ferment and will ideally last until the following summer, by which time it has acquired a literally eye-watering strength. It is imperative that enough cider be kept back for late winter and early spring, when the agricultural cycle requires the reciprocal *mingako* work parties that are held whenever a job is too big for one family to accomplish in a day: usually plowing a field or sowing a crop, but occasionally harvesting one, too. The workers are not paid, but work on the understanding that their effort will be reciprocated when they in turn need to plow, sow, or harvest. Another expectation is that they will be provided with cider throughout the day, and further cider when the day's work is done. The host places a carafe of cider and a glass in a furrow or on a fencepost, and the workers take it in turns to offer the glass around to their peers. It doesn't take long for the wasps to smell the sweet air and come circling. And frequently, in their wake, come one or two drinkers who simply sit and provide a sporadically coherent commentary on the work. These drinkers are served food and drink alongside everyone else, their comic accompaniment an integral part of what makes a *mingako* function.

Growing up in Britain in the closing decades of the last century, I'd come to understand cider as being clear, sweet, smooth, and fizzy; strong, for sure, but not harsh to the palate. The hazy, murky, vinegary cider here was a wholly different undertaking, though: nothing like the industrially produced stuff back home. It was sharp and rough, but full of a taste reminiscent of both the apple it had once been and the undone mass of sugars and microbes it was fast becoming. There was sediment and the inevitable drowned wasp or two at the bottom of every glass, but it grew on you with each sip. People, especially men at work, frequently proclaimed their great thirst for cider: to warm up when it was cold and to cool down when it was hot. I, too, acquired a taste for this cider, despite the still-raw scars of my teenage cider consumption. One could become a connoisseur, an enthusiast, because different apples, distinct containers for fermentation, and distinct periods of fermentation all produced distinct tastes. One of the chief drawbacks (or perhaps benefits) of this rustic cider is that it can be very strong, especially by the time it reaches full fermentation in late winter. It is then that you learn one of this cider's more peculiar features: the hangover arrives well before sobriety—you can be merrily drunk and simultaneously feel hammer blows to your head, accompanied by a burning sensation all over your skin.

The joys and woes of cider aside, it was something that all families needed in order to get through the year, a necessary prerequisite for the communal labor that even teetotaling Pentecostal families required. Hence, our previous day's endeavors at picking up apples off the ground under the small orchard that was nestled next to the pines between Juan and Marta's homestead and the shore of the lake. Traditionally, in Mapuche society, apple trees do not necessarily belong to the owner of the land, nor do all apple trees in an orchard necessarily belong to the same owner. In this case, the land was leased to Juan and Marta, but most of the apple trees where we were gathering were retained by Juan's Aunt Mercedes, a staunch but friendly Pentecostal convert. Yet despite Mercedes being the recognized owner of these trees, there was something of a gray area as to who owned the apples that had already fallen off a tree. Was it the owner of the apple tree? Or the owner of the land upon which the apples had fallen? We went for the latter interpretation, and the odd accidental shove of the apple tree augmented our haul. All of us, from youngest to oldest, spent several hours filling salmon-pink potato sacks with apples, until the oxcart was loaded with several hundred kilos.

When we finally arrived at Kod-Kod's the following day, we patiently waited our turn at the head of a long wooden channel set up on the dirt patio behind his house. The press consisted of an old car jack that slowly brought one metal plate down onto another, squeezing the juice out of the apples, which were held in place by the sacking. The juice would then flow down the long wooden channel, picking up a few extra wasps as it did so, until it could be decanted into the relevant container at the far end. There was something of a festive atmosphere at the press, as people from different communities around the lake finished off the dregs of the previous year's production. When our turn came around, Camilo asked me to take his photograph holding up jugs of the fresh, newly pressed juice. Almost immediately, Kod-Kod was upon me. "No, no, no! This is my press and I don't want any white people taking photographs and making money off me!" Kod-Kod's concerns were not entirely unfounded; it was indeed the case that photographic images of Mapuche people sold well as postcards in the tourist markets of Temuco, Pucon, and Villarica and extremely unlikely that the subjects of these photos received any recompense for them. I should of course have let the matter go, but a couple of hours of drinking year-old cider on one of the last warm days of summer hadn't really opened my eyes to the broader contexts of the politics of representation. "I'm taking a photo of the kid, not your cursed press. And you don't own that kid," I said. It was such a slurred, ill-formed argument that Kod-Kod just smiled and said, "Well, okay, but if I find my press on a postcard, I'll find you and I'll kill you." From that moment on, Kod-Kod and I were friends.

His real name was Juan Fernando Huenchumilla, but even his own family just called him Kod-Kod. The Huenchumillas of the island addressed the Huenchumillas of the isthmus as cousins, but they were in fact not related. As Esteban once explained to me, the ancestor of the island Huenchumillas had been a Curiqueo, but having served as a *kona*, a man-at-arms, to the great *lonko* leader Pascual Huenchumilla, this man became known as *Pichi Huenchumilla*, "Little Huenchumilla," the name his descendants still bear today. The two extended Huenchumilla lineages were aware of this connection, and for this reason there was always a strangely paradoxical air of intimacy and aloofness in relations between them. Perhaps this is why Juan seemed a bit surprised when Kod-Kod invited us into his house, away from the crowd around the press.

Kod-Kod was a good-looking man, with bright eyes and with a red baseball cap permanently attached to his head. Over the years I knew him, he always seemed to locate himself above and beyond the immediate social context and peer down from a great height, like a hawk, before descending to pounce with a cutting comment or joke at somebody else's expense. He was warm and yet wary, generous but calculating. We drank pisco and cola and talked long into the night. He repeated his warning about theft, the theft of images. "We know that that is what white people do, they steal even when they don't know they're stealing! *Weñefe kom!* All thieves!" I would have felt embarrassed, nervous, or even threatened but for the coarse cider layered with pisco sitting in my belly, soaking into my blood. I assumed that he was talking about other people, and unconsciously yet conveniently excused myself from the entire debacle of European colonialism in the Americas. Kod-Kod continued, "I went to Santiago and they robbed me. I went to Temuco and they robbed me. And they come here robbing us, taking our land, taking our pictures." "But I'm not like that," I objected, for it took me a further twenty years to realize that of course I was and still am exactly like that, perhaps not in as direct a way as Kod-Kod imagined—but I'd taken more than I could ever give, that was for sure.

A few years later, a friend phoned to tell me the news of Kod-Kod's death. He had been driving a tractor pulling a trailer-load of people back to the island from a football tournament next to the sea. Rather than go the long way around to the permanent bridge to the island, the tractor had attempted the steep descent to the ford, skidded in the treacherous mud, and overturned, crushing Kod-Kod and his young nephew in the cab of the tractor. He was a year older than me. Many will still not descend by the ford at night for fear of the astuteness of Kod-Kod's ghost.

*   *   *

Growing up in the city, the stars always appeared muffled to me, seen through gauze, an almost dainty presence that I usually ignored. But walking out at night onto the small hill behind Juan and Marta's homestead, the sky seemed to me alive, bristling with energy and light. The huge speckled band of the heavenly river, the *wenu lewfu*, reached overhead from horizon to horizon. Either side of the river's milky path, the sky shimmered through different colors: purple, terra-cotta, deepest blue. Rather than being faint pinpricks of light, the stars coalesced and condensed, turning the heavens into mottled patches of black and white, like the cows stretched out in the field below, munching even in their sleep. It was hard to see this and not be sucked in, not be drawn to the architecture of shapes, patterns, and forms circling slowly overhead, changing course nightly, weekly, monthly. So I did the thing all good scholars should: I bought a book. Or more accurately, I got my mother to buy a book and a few weeks later, I took the bus into the port to pick it up from the mailbox I shared with Esteban.

It was an atlas of the southern night sky, maps of all the great constellations cross-referenced with an astronomical calendar. It showed me all of those patterns so strange to me, so familiar to others: the Southern Cross, the Corona Australis, and all the northern constellations turned upon their heads. I hoped that I could somehow turn my newfound interest in astronomy into something resembling what is sometimes called "ethno-astronomy," the exploration of non-Western astronomical knowledge. Before coming to Chile, I'd read a book about the dark star constellations of the High Andes, where the light of the Milky Way is so bright that what stands out are not the stars themselves but the opposite, the dark patches in their midst. Entire agricultural and ritual cycles are mapped onto the passing of these dark shapes through the night sky. It seemed like a good subject to pester people about: innocuous, straightforward, but interesting all the same.

Yet nobody seemed to know anything. One or two people might know the name for the odd constellation, but no one seemed to have any kind of systematic knowledge of the stars in the way I had imagined. With hindsight, I see that I'd envisaged Mapuche knowledge as a kind of veneer on top of a self-evident and predefined objective reality, a reality that, not coincidentally, corresponded neatly to my own cultural knowledge. Thus, I'd imagined what a future academic production might call "Mapuche ethno-astronomy" as simply an alternative set of labels for the same basic constellations. What I came to understand was that what is usually translated from Mapudungun as "knowledge," *kimun*, was as much about not knowing as knowing; that a growing awareness and acceptance of ignorance was the teleology and pedagogy behind it: you learned to know that you did not know. Such an understanding of knowledge emerged from a world constituted not of objects, but of forces. Once I'd understood this, I came to approach the night skies in a different way, focused not on the movement of fixed patterns but on the cosmos as an ever-pulsing force.

After *once*—an evening snack of bread, jam, and *mate* tea—I took to trudging up the hill behind the house. There, I would lie on my back and attempt to align the stars in the sky with the stars in my atlas, peering at the pages using a tiny penlight. On occasion, I would drag a rather reluctant Juan up there with me and pester him with questions about comets, dark clouds, galaxies, and the moon. He'd just laugh and tell me that he didn't know anything. I see now that I'd failed to understand what *kimun* really meant. For the people I was living with, knowledge was not something set apart from our experience of the world; it couldn't be objectified, it couldn't be reduced to a set of labels to be affixed to all the things of the world. *Kimun* is primarily about cultivating an openness or sensitivity to the forces that constitute the world. You can understand these as lots of different forces, or as a single force that manifests itself in different ways. Mapuche people call this force *newen*. Sometimes I imagined *newen* as a deafening roar, the force of all existence screaming in one's ear. At other times, I imagined a perfect empty silence from which things coalesced and emerged for brief moments before returning to silence. Another way of imagining force is reflected in the beauty of Mapuche place-names, most of which are onomatopoeic. It's almost as if the places are naming themselves, declaring their existence and bringing it into being: *Traytrayko*, "the water that says tray-tray"; *Rawkenwe*, "the place where the waves crash saying raw." The birds, too, call out their own existence: *run-run*, the bird that cries "run-run," *tregül*, the bird that cries "tregul," and so on.

One of the features of this world of forces is that knowledge sometimes takes the form of ignorance, or at the very least the idea that knowledge isn't opposed to ignorance. The world isn't a static thing about which one can accumulate ever-increasing detail. It is in a constant state of flux, and knowledge is about being aware of those fluctuations, realizing that what one thought one knew could collapse in a second. Walking with people over their land, land they'd been born on, land they'd spent their entire lives working, I came to realize how heterogeneous, even fickle, the land could be—how some places were never really knowable.

Perhaps one of the most vivid instances of force was the moon: as they do all over the world, the phases of the moon push and tug at all of life here. The tides caused by the moon are not confined to the sea but extend to the very blood coursing through our veins, to the surge of life through a sprouting seed, to the sap running through an old tree. And for human action to be effective, it has to be working with rather than against these surges. Thus, people take care to observe the moon: to note its fullness, its waxing, and its waning. Esteban would often carefully arrange the date of a risky operation, such as castrating a stallion, in accordance with the phase of the moon. Some tasks were best carried out when the moon was at its strongest, just before it came into its fullness; others, when it was at its weakest, when its pull on the body's blood would be most negligible. This calibration of human labor with the oscillating force of the world applied not just to animals but to plants, as well. Decisions about the best time to sow a field of potatoes or to fell a great tree were all carefully aligned with the moon.

Of all the stars, my favorite is the Morning Star: the first to appear, the last to disappear. A point of light even once the darkness has gone and the sky turned to its clearest blue; and then a point of light again, heralding the return of night. One evening I was sitting with my elderly friend, Constanza, in her kitchen over on the island. The world seemed still and at peace. There was a faint breeze ruffling the line of eucalyptus below the house. The intensity of the sky's blue was increasing in anticipation of its turn to black. Constanza was a woman of dry wit; well-accustomed to the chaos and violence of men, she was always reticent, but when she did speak, it was usually a wry comment addressed at some man or other who'd overstepped the bounds of decorum. She was a hard person to speak to in any other register, for me at least. However, the calm of the evening seemed to have softened her, and as we sat quietly drinking *mate*, she asked me a question, a simple question: "How can it be that the star of the morning is the same as the star of the evening?" I didn't understand the question at first because, although she was speaking to me in Spanish, she used the Mapuche words for these things, "the star of the morning" and the "star of the evening." The former is *wünelfe*, "the bringer of the dawn," while the latter is *llepun*, literally "the sweeper," the star that sweeps the sky clean to make way for the night to come. As was so often the case during my years at the lake, my answer was unsatisfactory. I mumbled something about it actually being a planet rather than a star, but the truth was that I scarcely understood it myself. I was too busy recording her words in my head, noting these names for these versions of Venus, to really hear her question, to open myself up to my ignorance, or to see the beauty of the point at which her words and that solitary point of light intersected. I think of this star, and of Constanza, each time I hear the Litany of Loreto: "Gate of Heaven, pray for us. Morning Star, pray for us"—the beauty of Venus transecting the sky, the pioneer of the night, the herald of the morning.

I eventually lost interest in trying to map the stars, my failure to comprehend what knowledge really was for Mapuche people slowly becoming apparent to me. For *kimun* is not a set of facts about the world that can be memorized and then written down and possessed, but a capacity to attune oneself to the world. I realized that simply recording the labels of things was not getting me anywhere. I stopped pestering people for the names of the constellations, stopped worrying about planets, and began the slow process of letting my blood pulse with the moon, the Milky Way a cradle into which I was falling, the purple night giving way to its creamy light. Years later and thousands of miles away, I stood in the middle of the night on a Hebridean beach staring out into the Atlantic. In my hands I held a large lobster; a fisherman had given me a pair, and we'd eaten one but kept the other alive in the bottom of the fridge with the lettuce and moldering cucumber. But a pang of guilt caught me in the middle of the night and I decided to release it back into the sea. As I unraveled it from the damp tea towel in which it was wrapped, I paused at the recognition of those shapes, those colors; the creamy white stars spangled across its deep purple back, the stars of a distant southern sky reemerging across the other side of the world.

*   *   *

Esteban's brother, Alonso, asked me if I could give him a hand with his potato harvest. Potatoes are a staple crop across the south of Chile and have been so for millennia. Most of the Mapuche homesteads around the lake cultivated both potatoes and wheat for their own sustenance and for profit. The profit, however, was frequently elusive. Alonso had sown potatoes at a half-share on the land of a man whose name I think might have been Vicente, but whom everybody knew simply as Mish Amigosh. It was a strange nickname for sure, a deliberate mispronunciation of the Spanish *mis amigos*, "my friends." The nickname arose from the idiosyncrasies of his Spanish pronunciation and from his effusive greeting of any gathering of men. He was a kindly man, with an open and gentle face, yet always slightly nervous, a bit on edge. On the cold and graying day when Alonso and I arrived on horseback, Mish Amigosh was no different, already worrying that not enough people would turn up to finish digging the potatoes before the merchant's truck arrived. The price of potatoes could fluctuate wildly, doubling or even tripling in the space of a few days, only to crash back down to next to nothing a day later. For this reason, the harvest and sale of potatoes was often fraught with panic as people tried to cash in on good prices before they dropped.

Mish Amigosh had taken a gamble. He'd called the potato merchant in Carahue, the nearest agricultural town, and organized the sale of his harvest before he'd actually brought it in. The merchant's truck was due to collect the harvest that evening, and Mish Amigosh was literally begging people to help him. In addition to myself and

Alonso, there were maybe another five or six people working in the field. I am not a natural harvester of potatoes; I always seem to strike the hoe too near the roots of the plant, cutting the precious tubers in two and rendering them worthless. Whenever this happened, I would quickly kick some soil over the top to hide the yellowy white flesh and hopefully avoid reprimand. My other weakness was my height; within an hour, my back was killing me, and within two it was starting to spasm. But we all kept working away, filling the pink sacks with the red potatoes, each full sack weighing in the region of a hundred kilos. Some of the other harvesters would keep note of the number of sacks that they'd filled, because they'd been contracted by Mish Amigosh and were being paid by the sack. I, on the other hand, was working for free, or as Alonso put it to me, "for the experience."

By the end of the day, my hands were blistered and the soil had penetrated my skin, highlighting the lines across my palms and filling my nails. We all sat silently on the cool, dark soil in an exhausted stupor, waiting for the arrival of the truck and the cash. We didn't have to wait long; the truck pulled up to the entrance of the field just as the sky was deepening its blue into night and Venus emerged beyond distant trees. The driver of the truck was the merchant himself, a white Chilean with his head permanently pressed to a mobile phone, talking numbers, prices, and times. He was accompanied by two Mapuche teenagers who loaded up the heavy sacks as if they were filled with nothing but air.

It was getting dark rapidly and Mish Amigosh suggested that we, too, start loading the sacks onto the truck. For some reason, despite the fact that I wasn't getting paid, or perhaps because I was ultimately being paid for my participation in "experience," I suddenly felt obliged to help. Managing these sacks was not easy, with many of them weighing far more than I did. The idea was to swing the sack onto your shoulder and then run forward, all the while maintaining momentum. In order to get the sack onto your shoulder in the first place, somebody else took one end, you took the other, and together you swung it back and forth until it had enough momentum to allow you to dip your shoulder, swing higher, twist your whole body 180 degrees, and then lower the sack to a perfect balance across your shoulder. The first time I tried this, I turned the wrong way and wrenched the sack from my partner's grasp. On my second attempt, I didn't dip far enough and was hit full in the face by the hundred-kilo sack of potatoes, a trickle of blood emerging from my nose and lip. My third attempt was slightly more successful; the sack ended up more or less in place across my right shoulder. I could feel in my legs that I wouldn't be able to bear the weight for too long, so I started a delicate jog toward the truck, where a plank of wood had been laid from the ground to the truck bed. The plank was both narrow and at a steep incline; one really had to take a hard run at it to make it to the top, and this I did. Perhaps I'd got the angle wrong, or perhaps the very last drops of energy had finally deserted me, but after making it halfway up the bouncing plank, I crashed off the side into the back of the truck. The potato merchant found this hysterical, and his two assistants joined in the laughter, albeit more nervously—not quite sure what consequences laughing at this incongruous white stranger might bring. Had I had the energy, I would have punched the merchant there and then. As it was, I just slumped against the back of the muddy truck.

As I eventually picked myself up out of the mud, I realized that Alonso, the uncle for whom I was doing this favor, hadn't been seen for a while. And then on cue I heard his laughter coming from across the field. "*Malle, malle,* nephew, nephew, what are you doing? We thought gringos were stronger than that! It's just a sack of potatoes!" "So why don't you help load then?" I asked, less than amused. "I would, but I'm getting old and I have a bad back," he replied smilingly. I could see that there wasn't really much to win in this argument. "Come on," he said, "let's go to Tomás's and get a drink."

Whether he intended or not to invite all present, I don't know, but we all got to our feet and dusted ourselves off. By this time, the truck had been fully loaded, and Alonso joined Mish Amigosh in talking with the potato merchant. I don't know how much they got for the harvest, but they both seemed pleased enough, an increasingly rare occurrence at harvest time. Then we all wandered south across the fields toward Tomás's house. Tomás was Alonso's nephew, a very tall man, who despite being Mapuche had quite fair skin and blue eyes. I was constantly being confused with Tomás, or people thought I must be somehow related to him. Despite looking *winka reke*, "like a white person," however, Tomás was very much Mapuche. And he had a small lean-to shack off the back of his house where he sold all kinds of stuff, from toilet rolls to wine, It was the latter that we were after.

As I'd already discovered the previous year at Huacho's wheat harvest, exhaustion makes drink slip down more easily. This was sticky, sweet white wine in cartons—not chilled, but cold enough to feel refreshing after a day of work. Dark had by now descended completely and we stood around in a circle, drinking from a single glass in the usual fashion. Alonso and Mish Amigosh bought each other the first cartons, but from then on people bought and gave cartons sporadically, and the cartons soon seemed to circulate faster and faster, in an almost frenetic fashion. Beyond making you drink faster, exhaustion also seems to make you feel the effects of the alcohol faster, and several people were already a little unsteady on their feet. We'd reached the point where Tomás's wife wouldn't serve us anymore. As was often the case, Tomás hadn't wanted to get involved in the actual sale of wine; for Mapuche men, wine is nearly always given, never sold, thus its sale ends up being mediated by women. In this case, that was Tomás's not particularly enthusiastic wife. And as this source of wine seemed to have been exhausted, we decided collectively to move on. I remember only vaguely somebody having a truck, but I can remember with absolute clarity the shimmering of the stars as we headed further south, toward the sea at Inalafken.

It was only upon our arrival at some homestead or other in Inalafken that I remembered my horse, left tethered some miles back, near Mish Amigosh's fields. Alonso was gone, God knows where. We were still more or less coalesced as a group, standing outside drinking wine and cider, despite the fact that every one of us was pretty far gone. I wondered out loud how best to get back to the isthmus and the horse—the walk would have taken at least a couple of hours. A young man called Dani offered a solution. Dani was from the island in the lake and, as I discovered subsequently, did not have the greatest of reputations. What he was actually supposed to have done wrong was never made explicit, but people didn't trust him and always sought to avoid him. What I remember about him from that night is that he seemed sober and in control, rather than drunk and carefree like everybody else. Even at the time, this struck me as somewhat peculiar, maybe even slightly sinister, but I didn't pick up on these cues as much as I should have. Dani suggested that he hitch a lift back to the isthmus, pick up the horse, ride her back here to Inalafken, and then I could ride her all the way back home. For some reason, that made sense to me at the time.

We stayed there, drinking, but all I remember was noticing the moon slowly rising up and over our heads. The sight of the moon in motion made me feel that time had speeded up, that what felt like minutes were actually hours, but the dawn did not come. We were all from the isthmus or the island, and those of us still on our feet eventually started to feel that magnetic pull homeward. At some point, the potato merchant's truck pulled up, on its way back to the port after having gone to collect harvests further south, working throughout the night because of the rush to get the potatoes to market. We all piled onto the back, the pink sacks filled with potatoes feeling more comfortable than you might imagine, the cool smell of damp earth still filling the air. They dropped me near the school and I staggered home, forgetting the horse once again.

I was in a sleep so deep that the banging on the door to my room felt like it was a million miles and a million years away. Yet the feeling of not having any idea where I was or even who I was did not fill me with the usual momentary panic; it just seemed like an irredeemable fact of life. Marta's voice brought me back to the here and now. "They're looking for you," she said, both annoyed and amused. It was still dawn, a cold dawn that was creeping in the windows and under the doors. I couldn't find my trousers so I just stumbled outside into the biting morning wind in nothing but my boxer shorts, arms clasped around me against the world. It was Dani. In his hands he held the mare's reins, the mare shifting nervously from foot to foot, heaving her head up and down against the bit. "I went back, but you'd already gone," he said. I had neither the strength nor the will to argue; I just took the reins and walked away, back across the patio to a series of fence posts. There I removed the bridle from the horse. She was covered in a layer of sweat that seemed to be congealing into white scum on the surface of her chest and belly. I let her go, and she bolted off back up the hill.

For years after, Alonso claimed I'd broken the horse, broken her knee or ankle or hoof; that I'd lent her to a known reprobate who'd spent the entire night spinning her in *remolinos*, "whirlwinds," the equestrian equivalent of a handbrake turn or figure of eight, wrenching the horse around in the tightest circle possible. Doing this on gravel roads was a recipe for disaster. I would always keep silent and stare at my feet. I knew, and I think that Alonso knew too, that his real anger was with himself for selling me the mare in the first place in order to have money for drink. As for Dani, he avoided me. Some say he boasted of stealing a gringo's horse, of showing off his horsemanship. I don't know what's true. Whenever I saw him, he would slink away, disappear into the woods. The last I heard, he'd been killed, found facedown in the lake with his throat cut. My anger toward him had long since evaporated, and my guilt toward the horse had shifted to Dani himself. I see now that he had nothing and came to nothing, a life that was over before it had truly begun.

*   *   *

I can't quite remember why I'd crossed the deeply forested gully to Luis's homestead that morning. But I remember that I arrived just as he was leaving, sitting tall on a broad-chested bay horse, a horse with black stockings, as bays often have. He was heading out to see a small flock of sheep that he held *a media*, on a half-share, with a man named Huaiquimpan. *A media* in this context meant that Luis had contributed a few ewes the year previously, while Huaquimpan provided the pasture and care for the subsequent lambs to grow. Once the lambs were the right size, they would be divided equally between the two partners. This flock, however, had apparently been savaged by dogs, and thus Luis was setting out to assess the extent of the damage. He told me that he'd appreciate my company on the ride out, so I scrambled back to Esteban's house where I'd left my horse and then cantered around to the main road, where I met Luis fording the Llame stream.

Luis and I always addressed each other as *malle*, the term used between uncles and nephews. And there always was, and indeed still is, something avuncular about Luis. His hair was a dazzling white even back then, and he always dressed in typical Mapuche fashion for a man of his age: a battered trilby and a *makuiñ*, a heavy woolen poncho, over his shirt and trousers. Luis was wise in many things, and this wisdom came from quietly observing everything that went on around him. This quality earned him the not particularly flattering nickname of Frog, sometimes in its Spanish iteration, *Rana*, and sometimes in its Mapuche one, *Llüngki*. Luis's cousin Renato had named one of his own sons Luis in his honor. This younger Luis seemed to have inherited some of his namesake's powers of quiet observation, and it was not long before he, too, acquired the nickname Frog, although people now differentiated between *Pichi Llüngki*, "Little Frog," and *Füta Llüngki*, "Big Frog." As was often the case, nobody would dare breathe a mention of these nicknames in front of either of the two Luises, yet they were invariably referred to that way in their absence.

That morning, the elder Luis and I rode side by side along the gravel main road leaving the isthmus and heading south toward the beach at Inalafken, spurring our horses into the gorse bushes at either side when the occasional speeding truck or car passed us by, wary of the stones thrown up by their tires. After about an hour, we turned off down a path heading west toward the ocean and eventually came to a small house nestled amid native trees. A woman emerged, hair tied back in a bright headscarf wrapped around and knotted at the front. She had clearly been crying and seemed still distressed. She spoke swiftly and softly in Mapudungun. "*Üyew püle müley*," she cried, "They're over there." She went on to explain that Huaiquimpan, her husband, was away at the port on some errand. We guided the horses around the back of the house, dismounted, and looped the reins over fenceposts before heading down a slope in the direction the woman had indicated.

I hadn't really anticipated what a dog would do to a sheep. We came across the first body about two thirds of the way from the house to a small cluster of thick, dark trees. The sheep lay with its throat ripped out and its pale blue entrails spilling onto the dew-covered grass. Any hope of ours that at least some of the sheep might have survived depended on what lay within the grove of dark trees beyond. The thickest of the trees entwined with each other to form one end of a space no bigger than an average living room. Heavy vines between the remaining trees gave this arbor a horseshoe shape. At the far end, dead, mutilated sheep were piled up upon one another, herded into a corner, with their bloodied throats hanging loose. Every one of them appeared to have been disemboweled as well, like the first sheep, and flies already filled the air. We stood and looked; Luis poked at one with his boot. There wasn't really anything to say, but the silence and the smell of death made me feel like I had to speak just to feel alive. "They haven't actually eaten any of the sheep," I pointed out to Luis. He looked down as he answered, "They never do. They just get the smell of blood in their nose and keep killing. Dogs like that will never stop."

Huaiquimpan's wife—I never knew her name—was waiting for us at the wooden gate of the homestead as we returned from the site of the slaughter. She was now accompanied by a younger, larger woman who also had tears streaming down her cheeks. Neither of these women spoke Spanish, and Luis spoke softly in Mapudungun, addressing Huaiquimpan's wife as *fillka*, "brother's wife." "*Kimfali ti pu trewa?*" "Did you know the dogs?" he enquired. Both women shook their heads, "*Kimfalay*," they did not. But without recognizing the dogs, they could not seek compensation from the dogs' owner, and they also ran the risk that these same dogs would attack again. For a poor family like this one, the loss of the flock was a heavy blow. They would have invested a great deal of time and resources into getting the lambs to this point, almost ready for sale and the much-needed windfall that that would bring. And even worse than the material loss was the inevitable friction with neighboring homesteads that such an event would cause. This is the kind of event that so often leads to the fractures and fissures that frequently occur in any rural community: the pain of the loss and the uncertainty of whom, exactly, to blame. Luis was resigned to the loss, and I realized as we rode away that he hadn't gone there in search of a solution but rather to reassure himself that the attack was genuine, that his partner hadn't simply tried to sell off the flock on the sly. The renegade dogs were too far away from his own animals to pose a real threat, and his lack of questions suggested to me that he already had a clear idea to whom the dogs belonged. However, the price of the disrupted relations that would follow from pursuing the issue was too great; he smiled faintly and turned his back upon the whole affair as we headed back toward home.

We were quiet as we rode back, each of us engrossed in our thoughts, mine of blood and the cruelty of dogs, Luis's about I don't know what. After we forded the Llame stream and started up the gravel slope to home, Luis started to talk of the winds and the stars. This kind of information was what I was hungry for, the kinds of things I once thought I needed. And Luis knew this and gave it to me as a gift. He told me of the *puelche*, the east wind, the *waywen kürüf*, the south wind, and of all the winds that bore down upon the land. For many older Mapuche people, the principal cardinal axis is not north/south, but east/west. All Mapuche houses are built facing east, ready to welcome the rising sun as it emerges from behind the distant purple haze of the Cordillera. Likewise, at the end of their lives, Mapuche people are buried facing the east. West lies behind them, the great Pacific Ocean, the *füta lafken*, the direction of death and misfortune. This quadripartite division can also be flipped on its side so as to divide the world vertically, with land, sky, ocean, and a fiery underworld, *Nag Mapu*, that produced the lava that would spurt from the great volcanoes to the east. When I'd read about this "Mapuche cosmovision" in earlier anthropological texts, or seen diagrams of it on posters and T-shirts for sale in the tourist markets of Temuco, it had seemed a like highly abstract schema, incomprehensible to most of the people whose lives it was meant to somehow represent. Yet listening to Luis, I could start to understand these structuring parameters of his world and feel the way in which everything was tied together, see how everything bore moral values of good and bad, life and death. I was happy—happy to have this information, but even happier that Luis had seen fit to share with me, to bring me within his *kimun*, his knowledge of the world. Yet I was also nervous, for reasons that I couldn't explain then but now perhaps understand better: I knew that I could never really understand what was being offered, could never really live it or feel it as instinctively in my body, as a wind's whisper over my skin. I was aware even then that I would turn it into something just as abstract as those ubiquitous diagrams of Mapuche cosmovision that adorned countless tourist T-shirts. And I would come to stare at what I had written just as I stared at those dead sheep, wondering what was missing: all the parts were there, but the blood pumping through their veins was gone and their eyes had glazed over.

We parted at the top of the hill, Luis turning back southward to his homestead and I continuing along the main road northward to mine. A cold wind rolled in from the ocean, and the birds stopped calling.

*   *   *

I'd come unstuck moving from the city to the country; my friends came unstuck moving in the opposite direction, from the security and familiarity of rural life at the lake to the loneliness, isolation, and exploitation of the city. They didn't go there unaware of these dangers, for life at the lake was full of stories about returned migrants that highlighted every imaginable way people could be abused, swindled, and screwed over. But for young people growing up in the claustrophobia of small, overcrowded homesteads desperately trying to make ends meet through the monotonous and interminable cycles of agricultural labor, the lure of the city was powerful. The beauty of the rising sun over the distant Cordillera or the setting sun over the Pacific's mighty breakers didn't have the same hold over those for whom it was the only dawn and dusk they'd ever seen. And there was, of course, the money; nobody at the lake really had any, but those returning from Santiago always seemed to have it in abundance, rolls of banknotes spilling out of their pockets. The great city, the *futa waria*, had been a cardinal point in the Mapuche imagination for decades. An entire new generation had been born and raised there, and now a third generation is forging a new kind of Mapuche existence in the heart of the city, with often but a passing glance back to the southern heartland of their grandparents.

Traveling between Chile and Europe, I would inevitably have to pass through Santiago, yet I never really embraced it as I had done other cities. Maybe I'd absorbed too much of my Mapuche friends' antipathy toward white Chileans, *winka*, or perhaps back in those days it really wasn't that nice a place. More recent visits have revealed to me a whole new city, and I'm left wondering where all of these beautiful

barrios and lovely parks were hiding when I was passing through
before. The answer probably lies in the fact that back then I'd always
stayed with friends from the lake, people whose poverty dispersed
them to all of the most deprived fringes of the city, scattered across
a huge, sprawling, and ever-expanding urban mass; pushed further
away from the white elites snuggled against the foothills of the Andes
and closer and closer to the arid valleys to the south and west. They
rarely lived in the barrios that were served by the capital's metro system and instead relied on the impossibly slow buses to move around,
often commuting for more than two hours each way to reach their
poorly paid jobs. Most of the men worked either in bakeries or construction, while the women worked as maids, either live-in or live-out.
The women's work seemed more secure, with greater benefits, but they
nevertheless seemed to come off worse in the city: so often seduced by
the apparent glamor of the white boys of the city, their accents, their
jokes, so different from the quiet reserve of the Mapuche boys with
whom they'd been raised. A new generation of children with Mapuche
mothers and *winka* fathers slowly trickled back to their grandparents
in the rural south, at first startled at the ways of the countryside, the
knife through the chicken's neck, the blood of the slaughter, their confusion at the strange language coming from their grandparents' lips.

Their confusion in the south mirrored mine in the capital. I
would wander the streets off the Alameda—the city's spinal cord—
and become lost in a world of gray confusion. In a country with relatively little in the way of regional accents, Santiago is the exception
to the rule. With its strangely high, rising pitch, syllable after syllable
simply disappearing off the ends of words, I could barely understand
anything anybody said to me. Once, trying to take a shortcut around
the back of the central station, I stepped up onto a cardboard box to
get out of the way of a street cart peddling children's dolls. The box
gave way beneath me and turned out to have been brittle polystyrene
rather than cardboard. Its irate owner soon appeared, explaining that
this was his livelihood, the box that he used to carry the ice lollies that

he sold from bus to bus in the sweltering heat of summer. A friend of his soon arrived as well. "You have to compensate him. You have to give him the money to buy a new box," he asserted, inching his face toward mine. I pointed out that the box had been left in the middle of a busy pavement, forcing people to step over or onto it, but this seemed to be beside the point. I finally relented and agreed to buy him a new box. "How much?" I asked. "Twenty thousand pesos," was the reply. I laughed; I knew that such a sum was literally ten times the cost of the old polystyrene box. I didn't even bother to argue but gave him a five-thousand-peso note and walked away, the man's friend continuing to harangue me and demand ever more ridiculous sums. This all just confirmed what my friends at the lake had constantly warned me about: they will swindle you, they will trick you, they will take you for all you're worth. My Mapuche friends, they explained, were at least somewhat protected by their poverty: it was usually clear that they were barely worth swindling unless it happened to be payday. I, on the other hand, was clearly a gringo tourist who by definition held untold riches.

I would stay with my friend Javiera, in her lodgings in La Legua, a suburb of Santiago. The lodgings consisted of a couple of rooms in a lean-to garage at the side of a house. Her two brothers, the twins Pitu and Jony, and Pitu's wife lived there too, as well as Javiera's son Franklin. We all slept in one room, which, in the heat of summer, I wasn't really used to. Some kind of strange bedbugs left blisters all over my back and shoulders which then rubbed against the sweat-soaked cotton of my T-shirt until they burst. I was really only there because of Daniela, Javiera's younger sister, the young woman with whom I'd become so smitten and whom I'd embarrassed with my dancing in the fire at the lake. Over twenty years later now, I can't really explain why I was so smitten with her back then. History happens first as tragedy, then as farce, as Marx once wrote.

During the day, everybody went off to work, apart from ten-year-old Franklin, who'd either go to school or watch cartoons on TV. But in the evening, people would gather to drink, talk, and dance. I have happy memories of those sunny days, at the side of a garage in a dusty Santiago barrio, but always tempered with an ever-present anxiety.

Daniela, it soon turned out, was pregnant. She'd been seeing a very short white guy whom I alternately referred to as Enano, "the Dwarf," or Payaso, "the Clown." I guess it was fairly evident that I didn't like him much. I recognized in him those boys I'd once known in school, boys who managed to convince people that everything about themselves was familiar and normal, while everything that was different from them was strange and perverse. They worked their charm by drawing others into their world and raining vitriol on everybody else, weaponizing their own small-mindedness. The Dwarf did this through his whiny Santiago accent, his constant use of obscure Chilean idioms that none of us understood, and his never-ending references to how great Chile was. He would force us to watch *Había una vez*, a sports show that celebrated the greatest moments in Chilean sporting history. This was in the days before Chile's national football team had actually managed to string together some decent performances, and thus the "greatest moments" often amounted to things like the time Chile came third in the 1973 world spearfishing championships. I could barely suppress my sniggers as we sat and watched this crap.

Of course, much of the Dwarf's vitriol was directed against me, somebody who was clearly not a Chilean and could never be wrought into one. But my Mapuche friends were a different case, as from the perspective of a lot of white Chileans, Mapuche people are either failed Chileans or somewhat diluted Chileans—they had the potential within them to be proper Chileans, if only they could see it! The first step along this road was to either deny or ignore anything distinctive about them. The highbrow iteration of this was the claim by the renowned Chilean historian Sergio Villalobos that Mapuche people didn't actually exist but were really just "Chileans of Araucanian descent." This would have come as something of a surprise to the

1,745,147 people who identified themselves as Mapuche in the 2017 census, not to mention the further 205,009 Mapuche on the Argentinean side of the Cordillera. The more popular version, espoused by people like the Dwarf, was to constantly state that "we're all the same blood, we're all just Chileans," and that the people who were fighting for the return of stolen Mapuche land were "just terrorists, communists, and troublemakers," most probably manipulated and stirred up by foreigners like me. This was a common trope; earlier that year, I'd been at a community meeting concerning a proposed new highway to circle the lake, and the Regional Planning Minister asked me if I was there "to instigate revolution among the Indians," happily saying this in front of everybody present despite the fact that *indio,* "Indian," is considered, by Mapuche people at least, to be a deeply racist and offensive term.

This kind of patronizing nationalism pervaded Chilean public life. Inconvenient facts—like the presence of more than two hundred thousand Mapuche across the border in a rival nation-state—were simply ignored or obscured. A few years previously, my friend Esteban had taken part in a television documentary that recreated a journey on horseback that his grandfather had once made, from the lake nestled up against the shores of the Pacific, all the way across the continent, to Buenos Aires on the shores of the Atlantic. The purpose of the initial trip had been to plead for the release of Mapuche prisoners of war, following their defeat in what was known in Argentina as the "Conquest of the Desert." In recreating this epic voyage, Esteban, two companions, and a film crew also crossed the Cordillera into Argentina on horseback. Arriving at a small Mapuche community in Neuquen, the far side of the mountains, they filmed an encounter with an old woman who spoke to them in Mapudungun of *kiñe mapu müten,* which could be translated as "just one land" or, more politically and aspirationally, "just one nation." The inclusion of this brief statement in the final edit was enough for the television channel to refuse to screen the documentary, labeling it "antipatriotic" and overly political.

As I have already mentioned, many Mapuche people in the city become absorbed into this nationalist narrative, ceasing to be Mapuche and becoming instead simply *sureños*, "southerners." But my general antipathy toward the Dwarf, most likely fueled by beer and pisco, meant I wasn't going to let him exclude me so easily. If I was doomed to be a failed Chilean, then so was everybody else! This all came to a head one sultry evening in February, at the height of the southern summer, during a brief visit to the capital. My utterly cynical strategy was just to speak to Pitu in Mapudungun. At first he was reluctant, claiming that he didn't really know anything, but as the drink flowed, he relaxed into the tongue in which he'd been raised. I seemed to have inadvertently let a genie out of a bottle; as Pitu spoke, he became more and more irate at the daily indignities he was subjected to by *winka*—their rudeness, their stinginess, their racism, their lack of respect. The Dwarf could see where all of this was heading and took direct action. He leapt up from the table, spilling countless bottles of lukewarm beer as he did so, and screamed "I hate you!" at me. This was followed by a string of pure, unadulterated Santiago insults, so quickly that none of us could quite grasp what they referred to, but the intent was clear enough. Drunk by then, I just sat and laughed. The Dwarf then grabbed me by the collar and dragged me outside, which made me laugh even more uncontrollably. Daniela was trying to drag him away by his left arm, but he raised his right to strike me. At this point, Pitu, still in full *weichafe*, "warrior," mode, grabbed the Dwarf by his throat, threw him to the ground, and then sent him on his way.

I won the battle, but I lost the war. In fact, it turned out that I'd actually lost the battle, too. "Why didn't you hit him? Why did you let him speak to you like that? What kind of man are you?" were the questions directed at me once we were back in the house. Daniela looked at me disappointedly. She would go on to have that child and another by him, before he left her for another woman. Looking back, I know that I never had any future with her anyway, but the shame and indignity still burn. Not so much the shame of defeat but the shame of having ever thought that I had a place in these peoples' lives in the first place. With hindsight, I can see that it all felt too much like a game without consequences for me, but for them it had whole lifetimes of consequences.

*   *   *

There are some things that you can clearly recognize as political: extrajudicial killings by the police, hunger strikes by political prisoners, the dawn raids used by the Chilean state to terrorize Mapuche communities, and the omnipresent technologies of surveillance. But there are other things that flatter you into overlooking both their political nature and your own not-so-innocent place in that politics. Language was just such a thing, seducing me and hiding itself behind layers of authenticity and ignorance.

Most of the people I lived with around the lake spoke the Mapuche language, Mapudungun, a language unrelated to any other South American language and famous among linguists for the complexity of its verbal constructions. In Mapudungun, the verb seems to voraciously consume any surrounding nouns, pronouns, and adverbs, resulting in mind-bogglingly long words. There was a kind of continuum of linguistic juggling among the people with whom I lived, with those at one end, mainly elderly women, speaking just Mapudungun and very little Spanish, while those at the other, mainly young people and perhaps raised in the city, speaking just Spanish and very little Mapudungun. The vast majority were in the middle, perhaps more comfortable in one or the other language, but equally capable of understanding and responding in the other. As is often the case, this linguistic shift mapped onto generations, so that while all of the older people spoke Mapudungun as a first language, most of the younger generation were happier speaking Spanish.

I wanted desperately to learn to speak Mapudungun. It seemed to me then to be the key to a deeper, more authentic understanding of

what being Mapuche meant. It also seemed at the time to be a disciplinary requirement for an anthropologist, a badge of honor, to speak
a non-European language. I'd managed to get hold of a textbook for
learning Mapudungun from a member of the Summer Institute of
Linguistics (SIL), a somewhat controversial evangelical association
dedicated to translating the Bible, or at least the New Testament, into
all of the world's languages. Frequently accused of being conspirators
in US imperialism, the SIL sent its missionary-linguists around the
world to translate the Bible, as well as to bring local people everywhere up to a level of literacy sufficient to engage with the text in their
respective languages. The SIL member that I met was just heading
back to his native Kentucky after spending nine years translating the
New Testament into Mapudungun. To this day, I'm awestruck at this
task, not sure whether to describe it as Herculean or Sisyphean—the
former for its scale, the latter for its almost complete inutility: because
to this day, scarcely any of even the most committed evangelical
Christian Mapuche have literacy skills in Mapudungun.

   With my textbook in hand, I took to studying. In the evenings,
once the cows had been brought in, I would sit at the dinner table
and try out my new vocabulary and grammatical structures on Juan
and Marta. It was disconcerting to me, to say the least, that neither of
them seemed to understand a word I said, even though both of them
were native speakers of the language. What was I doing wrong? Was
it my pronunciation? My syntax? Eventually, I realized that this was
probably down to at least a couple of factors: regional differences,
for one, and the fact that I was producing chunks of discourse completely out of context, for another. There was, however, a third factor,
which I could never really appreciate until a few years later. This was
simply the fact that it was completely incongruous and bewildering
for a white person to speak Mapudungun. In those days, for many
rural Mapuche people, speaking Mapudungun was not necessarily
a source of pride, a gift to be treasured and handed down to their
children, but rather a stigma, a mark of shame. It identified them as

backward and as occupying the bottom rung of Chile's racial hierarchy. This pervasive racism was absorbed in many different ways,
but so much of it was through a self-inflicted negation. Thus, many
people I knew, fluent and gifted speakers of a beautiful and complex
language, would dismiss it as "slang" or "dialect," or justify speaking
it only because they "couldn't speak Spanish very well."

I was once sitting in Sebastián's kitchen, over on the island, talking
to his nephew, who was also called Sebastián but known universally
as Merengue for his idiosyncratic dance moves, and mentioned previously for his attempted theft of a bedraggled, dead coot. He was
the only son of a woman who spoke only Mapudungun, and as such
it is fair to say that he was a native speaker of the language. I always
tried to speak to him in my broken Mapudungun, frequently realizing my many errors just as the errant words escaped from my mouth.
After one such error—I can't remember exactly what—he looked at
me in wonder and said, without a trace of irony, "Ah, so that's how
you're supposed to say it. All these years my mother and I have been
saying it wrong." I was confused at first, then somewhat elated that
my Mapudungun was so passable that Merengue could believe that
about me—but then, finally, dismayed. Dismayed because I could
now see that I was not so isolated, not so innocent from the politics
of race as I'd imagined myself to be. I lived with Mapuche people, I
ate and worked with Mapuche people, I'd endeavored to learn their
language. But for people like Merengue, I would always be *winka*,
a usurper, not necessarily in a derogatory or uncaring way but in a
way that cast me as simultaneously superior and inferior: superior in
terms of money and power, inferior in terms of moral worth. Race
is a complicated thing, and perhaps nowhere is it more complicated
than in South America, where racial identities seem to be constantly
morphing and blending into one another, where ethnic identities
seem to swap places before one's very eyes, where the same person is
white one minute and Indigenous the next. For people like Merengue, being Mapuche was not solely about the color of one's skin or the

language one spoke but was also inextricable from a particular moral identity, one that emphasized respect and sharing in ways that the white people they encountered rarely displayed or even understood.

There were official attempts to increase people's engagement with Mapudungun or, better yet, to restore their pride in being speakers. These attempts involved at least three different and overlapping programs of Intercultural Bilingual Education that took place in the local primary school, two of which were funded by overseas funders. Working on one of these programs was how I'd come to the lake in the first place, in fact. And to my surprise, it had turned out that the biggest obstacle to the successful implementation of these programs was the parents, themselves speakers of Mapudungun. "We send our children to school to learn to become like white people. What good would learning Mapudungun be to them? Making them learn Mapudungun is white people's way of keeping us down!" explained one mother to me. I didn't know what to say; this wasn't the kind of response that the language activists I had met in the city had prepared me for. Over the years, I came to understand people's reticence to speak Mapudungun, their uneasiness in replying to my questions in Mapudungun, a little better. The color of my skin allowed me to speak Mapudungun without any fear of being mistaken for an "Indian," an abject figure of utmost discrimination at the bottom of every social hierarchy. While I could happily dabble in and play with the language, for them there were far-reaching consequences to its use.

Things, however, are changing. At the beginning of 2019, I received an email from Juan's middle son, Joaquín, asking me to send him a PDF of that same SIL textbook in Mapudungun that I'd acquired some twenty years earlier. He had started learning Mapudungun, despite now living in the regional capital, Temuco. It might seem strange at first that somebody who was born and raised in a Mapuche-speaking community, whose parents and grandparents are all native speakers of the language, might be asking an Englishman for a textbook written by Americans in order to learn that language. But such are the perversities of the politics of language. It is a start: ten years ago, Joaquín and his peers would laugh at the old people speaking Mapudungun; now they, too, want the language for their own.

*   *   *

The land gives, and the land also changes. The level of the lake always took me by surprise. Some of its changes were simply seasonal: the water level went up by a couple of feet in the winter and down by a couple of feet in the summer. Yet the fact that the lake would some- times breach the narrow barrier of land a few miles to the north and spill out into the Pacific itself made the water levels unpredictable even beyond the effects of these seasonal changes. One of the effects of this oscillation was that there was a strip of land around the edges of the lake that was sometimes underwater and sometimes not. This land provided rich pasture for cattle and sheep, but was also the hab- itat of a freshwater crayfish known in Mapudungun as *machew*.

The amount of effort and energy involved in gathering *machew* was rarely made up for by the meager nutrition they provided. Nev- ertheless, collecting them was both satisfying and fun. Successful *machew* hunting necessitated a holistic awareness of the land, the level of the lake, the firmness of the ground, the heat of the day, and so on. And like all worthwhile pastimes, it needed heavy investment in a gadget. In this case, the necessary gadget was a kind of home- made, hand-operated suction pump. A short piece of plastic piping was fitted inside another pipe of a slightly larger diameter, and a thin ring of rubber cut from a bicycle inner tube formed an airtight seal between the two. A vacuum would be created when the shorter pipe was pulled back. These devices were quite crude and never seemed to last more than one outing before the rubber gave way or the pipe cracked. Despite this, when the conditions were right, they could be quite effective.

One day, Joaquín had spent most of the morning tinkering with the pump, tying and retying the rubber seal, hacking old tires to pieces to extract still more strips of rubber, and attaching a wooden extension to serve as a handle. He had been thoroughly and intensely devoted to his task, and now seemed both confident and impressed with the final result, an optimism that was not shared by his mother, Marta, who told us flatly that we would catch nothing. A bright sun embedded itself in a sky of deepest blue as Joaquín, Camilo, and I wandered down through the great pines to the shores of the lake. Perhaps the word "shore" is a misnomer. What we actually faced was a small, daisy-strewn meadow that became increasingly muddy at its far side until it finally disappeared into a wall of high reeds; it was never quite clear exactly where the lake began and ended. A few black-and-white cows squelched knee-deep in the mud and gazed lazily in our direction, without pausing in their endless chewing. The reed bank behind them extended all the way to the island and held untold treasures. I would often gaze at this gently undulating wall for hours, hoping for a glimpse of a *siete-colores*, the many-colored rush tyrant, a small delicate bird of seven striking colors: red, black, white, blue, green, yellow, and gray. These birds flickered and flicked themselves through the tall graying reeds, rarely settling long enough for my hungry eyes to find them. The *run-run*, basically a blackbird wearing a pair of white spectacles, could also be spotted in the reed-beds, flying vertically three or four yards into the air, all the while making the distinctive call from which its name comes. For many, finally, the reedbeds' greatest treasures were the eggs to be found in the nests of the black-necked swans hidden deep within, to be gathered surreptitiously in the dead of night.

Once we'd reached the muddier section of the lake's terrestrial boundary, we separated and scoured the bank for the small holes that indicated crayfish burrows. Once Camilo or I had identified such a burrow, Joaquín would come over with his homemade device, position it over the hole, and pump furiously. Out would come a thick soup of mud and water, and mixed deep inside it would be the odd flash of pale orange speckled with red: the *machew*. For the most part, *machew* are fairly small, maybe just a bit bigger than your thumb. Nonetheless, their pincers can give a sharp pinch, so we were careful to grab them from behind as we scoured the newly extracted mud for our reward. Some burrows seemed to hold just one crayfish, but others seemed to hold two, three, or even more. Whether these burrows linked together underground, I have no idea. We kept the *machew* we'd caught in a big saucepan with a heavy lid, and the sound of their scraping and clawing at the metal was somewhat disconcerting, like a poltergeist shaking a rattle. After a couple of hours' gathering, we had a good half-panful of the scrabbling creatures, but the rubber seal on Joaquín's pump failed yet again, so we trudged back up the slope and through the pines to witness the *machew* meeting their fate.

Marta was waiting for us as we emerged from the dark trees into the light of the patio, a skeptical look on her face, which didn't diminish even after she'd taken the pan from us. We followed her into the kitchen as she placed the pan on the dresser without even opening the lid, the persistent scraping of the crayfish within creating a quiet undercurrent to the hisses of cooking already underway. Juan came in from the back field and immediately strode over to the pan, lifting the lid with boyish delight. "Wow, *machew*, wonderful! Marta, cook these up!" "Cook them yourself, there's not even enough to feed a child!" I was getting the impression that the passion for *machew* was something distinctly masculine, tied to the adventures and triumphs of boyhood. Grown adults, Marta implied, should know better than to waste their time and energy on such trivial morsels. For my part, I was still amazed, both that we'd caught so many and that it was even possible to literally suck crayfish from dry land.

Because Marta still refused to even contemplate cooking the *machew*, it fell to Juan to reach down the heavy frying pan and place it over the wood-fired stove. A bit of oil, some crushed garlic and chili, and then the contents of the saucepan were unceremoniously dumped into the frying pan. The frenetic scrabbling of red claws quickly subsided, and in only a couple of minutes Juan deemed the *machew* cooked. As you do with prawns or langoustines, you rip off the crayfish's head and claws and then, holding the carapace tightly, you can pull out the meat of the tail. It was sweet and salty, but with the earthiness of turmeric. Each crayfish was indeed small, but like a little jewel, its taste seemed to condense the entire experience. We all ate from the same pan, and soon enough all of the *machew* were gone.

Later that day, just as the sun was casting its final golden rays back toward the east from whence it had risen, I returned through the pines to the side of the lake. There were again cows munching distractedly, but different cows this time, brown-and-white ones, their brown turning a deep russet in the late light. They trampled the meadow, their heavy hooves coming down upon the burrows where the *machew* lived. I couldn't quite get my head around these aquatic creatures setting themselves up on dry land—did they just wait for the water level to rise again before emerging? Or would they leave their burrows at nightfall and scurry across the meadow, in and out of the hoofprints, until they reached water? There were many small mysteries to be found here at the side of the lake, a place in-between, growing and contracting, an almost tide-like oscillation with all of the mystery that the tides themselves entail.

*   *   *

Emiliano beckoned me over to sit with him and his two wives, sisters to each other. The high sand dunes behind us blocked our view of the great ocean, yet its continuous roar resonated all around us. The sinking sun, too, was obscured by the high sand walls, though an orange glow still filled the sky, ebbing away slowly as a deep purple encroached from the east. This was in the early days of my years at the lake, and I'd never met a man with two wives before. I remember feeling a flush of embarrassment course through me as I sat down on the woolen rug to join them. My own father married four times, so it wasn't the idea of multiple wives per se that shocked me, but rather their synchronicity. This kind of polygyny is now rare among the Mapuche; men with more than one wife are few and far between. And it was never common, the practice being restricted to *lonko* headmen—not exactly chiefs, but people whose responsibility it is to gather and maintain a consensus among staunchly autonomous households.

While the existence of polygyny was both amusing and titillating to many white Chileans, this reaction often felt hurtful to Mapuche people, who were keenly aware of how polygyny fed into racist discourses about their supposed savagery and lack of civilization. They knew all too well that the institution had emerged as a means of support in difficult times, nearly always a way of bringing an unmarried younger sister into the security of an established household (as we saw with Challa's parents in the previous chapter). Many people told me that the practice originated during the catastrophic late-nineteenth-century war that brought Mapuche independence to an end, the war euphemistically referred to by Chileans as "the Pacification of Araucania." That pacification led to huge numbers of Mapuche casualties and a subsequent dearth of young, marriageable men. Whether this origin story for the practice is true or not, I don't really know; many sources seem to suggest that polygyny far predated the war, but nevertheless, for the people I knew, it was a practice that carried within it the memory of colonial violence: that ultimately it was the greed of the white Chileans, the *winka*, that was responsible for the birth of polygyny.

We were there together to watch the horse racing. The small, nervous horses were to gallop along the broad stretch of flattened sand that was tucked in behind the dunes and shielded from the Pacific winds. The races had been organized by a committee that was raising funds for the electrification of the whole area, because, although the state would assume the bulk of the costs, individual families were too poor to install the necessary connections that would give them access to the grid. At that point, light was still being provided by the notoriously dangerous kerosene lanterns, from which several people had received horrific and life-changing burns, while the ubiquitous televisions ran off car batteries.

The committee collected money for the project from people for entering the races, but the real money was in the wagers placed between the owners of the two horses in each race. Huge sums of money were wagered, and given the enormous stakes riding on the results, it struck me that the beginning and end of each race were spectacularly vague and ill-defined. The horses were so wired—wheeling, bucking and straining, foam flying from the bit—that their riders struggled to line them up, and this process of trying to coordinate both horses to face the same direction seemed to go on for ten, twenty minutes. At some seemingly arbitrary point, somebody would decide that they were close enough, and they would fly off across the dunes. Perhaps not surprisingly, the result of each race was frequently disputed, and, again given the large amounts of money at stake, those disputes could quickly turn violent.

For this particular race, my eldest "uncle," my *malle* Amaro, was pitting a chestnut mare against a gray mare belonging to a man from Inalafken, further south along the coast. Both owners were backed up by an extensive network of kin, friends, and neighbors who all contributed to the stake. It felt to me like a team sport that had somehow been distilled into sweaty bodies of pure equine angst. The jockey was Amaro's son Lucas, a young man with whom I often played football. Not surprisingly, jockeys had to be small; not infrequently, people used children as young as seven or eight, seeking to place as little weight as possible on the horse's back and thus squeeze out even the most minimal of advantages. Lucas was not that much younger than me, but he was both short and slight, and happy that his diminutive stature was to his advantage for once. Each jockey wheeled his horse around and around in the sandy gravel, whipping it into a pure frenzy.

Spittle flew, eyes rolled up, and the horses reared until eventually, yet momentarily, they came into line. And they were off.

All of us milled around the starting point, gazing at the mares' narrow rumps as they disappeared into the distance. Night was falling fast, yet the start of the race had been delayed by the endless haggling over which neutral person would hold the wager while the race took place. From our vantage point, the horses seemed neck and neck, and as they eventually wheeled away from each other in the fast-descending gloom, we realized that we had no idea which horse had won. We would have to rely on the rival jockeys themselves to provide an answer, and predictably, they could not. I could see immediately that there was no possible way any result would be accepted as valid, but this didn't stop the crescendo of shouts, pushes, and gripes. Esteban's son, Juan Bautista, visiting from the city, surreptitiously picked up a large rock in preparation for the brawl that seemed inevitable. But it eventually emerged that due to the bickering about who should hold the combined wager, no money had actually left either set of supporters, and thus the situation could simply be ended by each party walking away with their money. Which they did, while trading everybody's favorite insults in Chilean Spanish. Swearing always seemed to work better in Spanish than in Mapudungun.

By now darkness had fallen, a final, faint western light evaporating over the ocean behind us. Seagulls soared and cormorants screeched as they headed to their roosts. A small generator was fired into action and a single bare lightbulb lit the scene like a tableau, a promise of the electricity that was to come one day soon. The generator was set up behind a small, makeshift shelter balanced on the sand: a few rough planks nailed together and a piece of corrugated iron over the top. This was where the real money would be raised for the committee, selling wine and beer once the racing was over. A pair of tiny, tinny speakers fed off the same generator and pumped Mexican country music into the cold Pacific night. I remember little of what followed. Emiliano brought me over to the shelter and handed me a carton of wine. He explained to me the precise etiquette of drinking—that everybody is served from a single glass that must always circulate counterclockwise (a procedure I would become very familiar with, as some of the stories I have already told make clear). The recipient of the carton refills the glass after each person has drunk, but each may drink as much as they want, from a small delicate sip to drinking the glass dry. This was new to me. I'd grown up where each man's relationship with his drink was both intimate and sacrosanct, where even touching another man's glass could lead to mayhem. Here, the various cartons and glasses circled around and through me at a dizzying pace. Each time the glass reached me, I took two big gulps before returning it, for I had noticed that the men on either side of me were doing the same. They were not, as it turned out, the best guides to initiate me into the subtleties of Mapuche drinking culture. Before long, everyone in our little circle of drinkers was swaying on their feet. The sensible ones, and the ones who were dragged away by their crying children or bored wives, left the rest of us there to drink on. The lightbulb swung in the wind and relentless songs of horses, betrayal, and Pancho Villa blared on.

I had initially come to watch the racing with Pablo, a political leader and also a friend, a big solid man with a big solid head and big solid hair, always laughing and smiling. And yet, despite his laughter and smiles, he was a friend with whom I never felt totally at ease, for his laughter seemed to barely disguise a resentment, or rather a bitter distaste—not for me exactly, but for what I seemed to represent to him. Pablo was from a local Mapuche family but had been raised in Santiago and been a prominent activist in leftist politics, the strand of leftist politics in which all the wrongs of the world stemmed from the United States. Given the infamous role the CIA had played in destabilizing Salvador Allende's Marxist government and ushering in General Pinochet's dictatorship in 1973, this was clearly not an unreasonable position, and it was one that was evidenced in Pablo's scars, both psychological and physical. The problem was that despite knowing exactly where I was from, Pablo kept insinuating and then insisting that I was a puppet of American imperialism and the CIA.

I could never fully understand his position, not because I disagreed with his politics but precisely because I shared them. I was, in fact, one of very few people around the lake at that time who appreciated his stance as a "Mapuchista," an activist for Mapuche rights. His attempts to persuade his neighbors that the Mapuche people should act as one, or that their interests were not represented by any of the mainstream Chilean political parties, were seen by most as irritating, misguided, and irksome. Many people dismissed him as a "terrorist," and his only friends were the small handful of other Mapuchistas in the area. What irked me was that despite this, he could never seem to see beyond my identity as a *winka* and, more particularly, as a *gringo*. Talking with Pablo, it was as if I personally had invaded Iraq and Afghanistan, killed Che, blockaded Cuba, and placed Pinochet at the helm of Chile. Every joke was at my expense, every critique of foreign affairs leveled at me.

That night I awoke with tufts of sharp dune grass sticking into my temple and cheekbone. A thin trail of vomit-stained saliva stretched thinly away as my face rose from the sand. I peered around me into the night. Three or four other bodies were dimly illuminated by the lamps of the shelter, twenty or so yards away. We were all *botado*, "thrown away." I pushed myself up onto my feet and Pablo peeled away from a small group of other men. He wasn't happy but, predictably, angry and embarrassed. I couldn't walk straight, so he put one arm around me out of necessity rather than affection, and we headed down the road home. The veil dropped; there was no laughter and no smiling; "Why are you here?" he asked me, "What is it that you want? Who do you work for?" Anthropologists struggle to explain what they're doing at the best of times, and this was not the best of times. "Studying culture," I slurred. "What culture?" "Your culture." "But what does that mean? What is it that you really want?" he retorted. "I don't know, I don't know," I confessed meekly. In fact, all these years later, I still don't know. What exactly was I doing? What did I want?

In all my subsequent years at the lake, Pablo never came to fully accept me. When my book was finally published, he told his neighbors that his suspicions had been confirmed, that I had written that all Mapuche women sleep with the Devil, that I had named them all as informants for this fact, and that I had earned myself millions in the process. None of these accusations was true, but what upset me most at the time was what I saw as the absence of any empathy on his part, his sarcastic refusal to accept me simply for who I was rather than seeing me as a makeshift token of white imperialism. Now, I see things differently; we are never "simply" anything.

*   *   *

Our nearest neighbors, apart from the elderly Valentina, were Luis and Isidora. They were both sharp-tongued, yet always ready to laugh, and thus fun to be around. Nothing passed them by. Luis was known as *Pichi Llüngki*, "Little Frog," to differentiate him from his uncle, the man with whom I'd witnessed the dog-ravaged sheep. And like his uncle, he was known for observing everything that happened, everybody who passed by; for registering the slightest shift in the social breeze. Visiting Luis was a little bit like skimming a local newspaper; he delivered all of the latest comings and goings in bite-sized reportages, with an added dose of sarcasm at no extra cost. Isidora, like Luis, was an astute observer of every little thing. She would somehow always know with whom I'd spoken, where I'd been, what I'd done. They were, by their own account, the poorest people in one of the poorest communities in what was, at the time, the poorest municipality in Chile. They owned only one hectare of land, far short of the fifteen deemed necessary for self-subsistence by the Chilean government. Yet Luis and Isidora did not consider the root of their particular impoverishment and marginalization to be located in the vagaries of Chilean colonialism and dispossession of territory, but rather in the fickle nature of the land upon which they lived.

One winter's day, we sat drinking dark brown beer in the kitchen of their perennially unfinished house. The house was a typical wooden kit house with a zinc roof, acquired through a government subsidy scheme, yet it remained open to the elements at its far end, where leftover materials from another building project had been commandeered to extend the living space. There had not been quite enough planks or cladding to ever finish the extension, so a southerly wind blew around our ankles as we sat discussing their problems, which turned out to have two distinct but interlinked causes. The first of these was the fact that they had to farm on the "foot" of the hill, which constituted the small scrap of land that made up Luis's only inheritance. But the "foot of the hill" means something quite different to people at the lake than its English equivalent would imply. Each hill is said to have four "feet" upon which it can raise itself up and, quite literally, walk away. This topographical mobility has both mythological and historical precedents. The well-known Mapuche origin myth of Treng-Treng and Kai-Kai tells of a battle between two great serpents, the former of which belongs to the land and the latter to the sea. Each time Kai-Kai raises the ocean up, its adversary Treng-Treng responds by raising up the hill upon which the original family—Old Man, Old Woman, Young Man, Young Woman—are taking shelter. In many versions, there is no final resolution to this conflict. Land and sea remain at war, and earthquakes are often said by local people to be the manifestation of the mythological battle in this world. Many small hills in the area are directly associated with, and indeed named after, Treng-Treng and share its capacity to get up on their four feet and walk away. This in fact occurred during living memory when, during the massive earthquake of 1960—the most powerful earthquake ever recorded globally—several hills "disappeared" due to the huge topological shifts. Thus, each hill is said to have four feet, one located in each corner, and to farm on one of these feet, whether intentionally or not, is to court disaster. It bothers the *ngen* spirit of the hill, just as a thorn would bother the foot of an animal. The ire of the hill becomes manifest in its withholding of fertility and its infliction of disease and failure on crops, animals, and people alike.

The second source of Luis and Isidora's problems was the fact that their house had been inadvertently constructed on a "demons' highway," a *weküfe rüpü*. These invisible roads, which crisscrossed the whole area, were used by a variety of malevolent beings to traverse the landscape, to get from one evil misdeed to the next. There was no shortage of sightings of mysterious horsemen, shining lights, and other denizens of the night at particular points along these "roads" that passed happily through forests, over ditches, across fields, and, in Luis and Isidora's case, directly through their house. The consequences of unwittingly building their house in the very middle of this demons' highway had soon been made apparent. From the beginning, every harvest failed, every agricultural subsidy was denied, every friendship turned sour. But worse was yet to come. For no apparent reason, their firstborn child weakened, faded, and died. Subsequent children survived, but the family could not find even the slightest relief from the perpetual poverty in which they found themselves. "Why don't you just move the house?" I asked, stupidly, as if such an obvious solution hadn't previously occurred to them. "Where would we go? This single hectare is all the land we have. They wouldn't give us another housing subsidy. Our only hope is that the demons switch paths."

The homestead was thus doubly damned, sited as it was on both the hill's foot and the demons' highway. These two problems blurred into one, the malevolent demons becoming indistinguishable from the supposedly more or less benevolent *ngen* spirit of the hill. "Nobody ever knows the land," Isidora told me, lifting my glass to wipe away the ring of moisture freezing to the table underneath. But to my mind, their confinement here was the result of yet a third damnation, the Chilean colonialism that had reduced the Mapuche from a huge territory, one that stretched across the continent from one ocean to the other, to the smallest patches of leftover land, the land that the white people didn't want to farm yet even now still seek to possess.

The world is composed of relations, and the realization that we have a relation with something is a prerequisite to truly respecting and appreciating it. This is what, according to Mapuche people, white people so often forget. But we would be mistaken if we assumed that this understanding of the intricate and embroiled relatedness of all things implies that all relations are good, beneficial, or nourishing. Sometimes Mapuche people, and indeed Indigenous people in general, are characterized as living "at one" with nature. This is not exactly true. What is true is that they realize that they are inextricably bound to the world, to the land, and to each other and, furthermore, that they are a part of the world, the land, and each other. They are in a "relation" with the nonhuman world—it sustains them, it nourishes them, it gives them delight—but, as Isidora and Luis knew all too well, it can also rip them apart, as mercilessly as a callous child slowly tearing the wings off a butterfly.

As I got up from the table that day to head home, Luis asked me for something. He literally said, "Can you give me something?" "What kind of 'something'?" I replied. "Anything," he said, "anything at all. Even the smallest thing." I was struck dumb by the question. I just didn't understand. "A picture, a key ring, a flashlight, anything," he continued. I mentally scanned my pockets and realized that I didn't have anything other than a bit of cash, and I thought that handing him that would be crude and missing the point, even more than I was already missing it. What they were asking for wasn't money, but a little piece of me. I told them I'd have a think about it and bring them something upon my next return. I never did.

Luis and Isidora understood better than I that they were in a relation with me; I wasn't simply an observer and they weren't simply objects to be observed. How could anybody possibly have been so blind as to have thought otherwise? Well, they knew from bitter experience that it was precisely *winka*, usurpers like me, who were capable of thinking otherwise, of seeing Mapuche not as people but as either an impediment to be removed or a resource to be exploited. A gift, no matter how small and insignificant to me, would be full of significance for them, a sign of my own acknowledgment of the relation that we were in and thus the possibility that unlike so many other relations, it could bear fruit. I never gave them anything. As cold and heartless as the demons racing by, I crashed through their house, through their lives, without ever pausing to understand, to relate. I went back last year, twenty years too late, bearing a gift, a large flag of Scotland's symbol, the Lion Rampant, to adorn their bare walls. But there was nobody home. The boys were all away working the vineyards a thousand miles to the north, the girls all maids in Santiago, and Luis and Isidora gone to the port to find out why, once again, their application for an agricultural subsidy had been rejected.

*   *   *

If you took the road south, you'd get as far as Tierra del Fuego, while if you took the road north, you'd reach Alaska. This was the impressive claim put to us one drizzly afternoon in a community building in the center of the isthmus by a gaggle of gray-suited men from the Ministry of Public Works. The specter of the much-discussed Coastal Highway was always in the background of any political discussion during my time at the lake. The Chilean state had proposed, and indeed started to implement, a grand project for a major highway to pass through the isthmus between the lake and ocean and thus "open up the area to development." All kinds of riches were promised: those whose land would need to be purchased for the widening and rerouting of the current gravel road would be compensated handsomely. And those whose lands were not directly in the path of the new highway would nevertheless benefit indirectly from the flood of tourists sure to descend upon the area, apparently desperate to consume the local "Indigenous heritage." Everybody would be a winner. The Ministry delegates genuinely hadn't anticipated why or how anybody might think that a highway going through the middle of their community and their ancestral lands would be a bad thing.

An old lady spoke up from the edge of the community hall. "We can't build a highway because it would pass through our ritual field, which belongs to God, and through our cemeteries, where we hold our dead." The gray-suited men rolled their eyes, smiled at one another, and drew heavily on their cigarettes. Then a younger Mapuche man spoke up. "We can't just do what we want with our bits of land. This land is part of all of us, and whatever we do with it affects all of us. Nobody has the right to just sell their land as if it were just theirs alone to sell." This was clearly too much for one of the younger Ministry officials, who pointed out that the whole point of private property was that people could buy and sell it as they saw fit. The old lady spoke again, this time getting to her feet: "Well, I don't know what 'private property' is but we just live here as part of the land. We belong to it, it belongs to us, and we can't sell it." The head official uncrossed his legs, took his feet off the table, and put out his cigarette. This clearly wasn't going as he had anticipated.

The usurper makes two errors: first, he mistakes relationships for objects, and second, he thinks that these objects can be owned by one person to the exclusion of everybody else. Not only does he make these two errors, but he has the vast machinery and legal apparatus of a nation-state to back him up and allow him to impose this skewed vision on everybody else, to enshrine it and protect it within myriad legal and political structures. Those who are *norche* insist on a different way of comprehending the world and, in both minor and major ways, resist this sad reduction of the world to nothing more than a collection of objects to be owned and fought over.

To be *norche* means to both see things clearly and act clearly. Its literal meaning of being "straight" or "direct" refers to the avoidance of obfuscation, confusion, and dishonesty. Mapuche people never needed Karl Marx to tell them that the concept of property conceals a social relationship. In fact, the Mapuche understanding extends the scope of what entities can constitute relationships far beyond what Marx could ever have imagined; land isn't just a relationship between people, but among a myriad flux of beings—spirits, trees, animals, the soil itself—all of which are already part of each other. This isn't to say that Mapuche people don't have desires for material things, nor that they can magically resist either the relentless consumerism that saturates the world or the exigencies of economic survival as some of the poorest people in Chile. But it does mean that they recognize that property is a contingent, fleeting thing. It was because they saw clearly just how strong the pull of money can be that the people of the lake felt compelled to present a united front. Much to the disgruntlement of the Ministry of Public Works, the local communities rejected the Coastal Highway and all it promised. Rumors occasionally surface that the project is being resurrected, but each new instance reinforces the people's determination to see clearly, to act clearly, as *norche*.

Postscript

L ife at the lake has changed in many ways since I lived there. The physical landscape looks much the same: the sun still sears blazingly down upon fields of golden wheat in the summer, while the rain still hurls itself relentlessly against zinc roofs and endless gorse throughout the autumn, winter, and spring. Stands of eucalyptus are felled, but more shoot up almost as quickly. Older wooden houses crumble back to the earth, yet new wooden subsidy houses are constructed just a few yards away. The social landscape, however, has changed almost beyond recognition. Nearly all of the young people I've written about here are gone: some dead, but most of them migrated to the cities or to the vineyards and orchards of the north. Many of the older people have died, and those who remain seem slower now, quieter. Despite the dearth of young adults, however, there are still lots of children, many of them the children of urban migrants who have been sent back to live with their grandparents, to help maintain the homestead and keep the land alive. There are more pickup trucks; once a rarity, now almost every other homestead seems to have one. And the televisions have gotten bigger. Marta complains to me that "everybody is too rich now. We're all so rich that nobody goes to visit each other anymore. When we were hungry and had nothing, we would visit our neighbors to borrow some sugar, some flour, eggs maybe. Now we have all the sugar and flour that we need. We never see our neighbors." And while it seems true that the continual circulation of people between homesteads has subsided, to my eyes at least the poverty remains all too visible in the broken houses, the broken faces, and the lack of opportunity that compels the young to leave.

Perhaps the biggest change is that life at the lake has become political in a way that wasn't visible before. Twenty years ago, most people at the lake subscribed to the notion that there were Mapuche people everywhere, in every corner of the world, and that, therefore, they had nothing special in common with the Mapuche communities in other parts of Chile's south who struggled against logging and ranching interests in the hope of reclaiming their stolen land. We would watch televised images of burning trucks, blocked roads, and demonstrations, and they seemed a thousand miles away. The communities around the lake seemed to exist in a bubble; everybody knew more about distant Santiago than about the Mapuche communities that were in conflict less than thirty miles away. The problems faced by those communities always seemed to be other people's problems. This, however, has changed. The people at the lake have now started to embrace the politics of Mapuche nationhood, to see themselves united—through language, culture, and belonging to the land—with others throughout the south, in the cities, and across the border into Argentina. The Mapuche flag, the *wenufoye*, can be seen flying proudly over many homesteads, when not long ago nobody would even have recognized it. Those protesting for the restoration of Mapuche lands are no longer dismissed as "terrorists" but understood to be *pu peñi, pu lamngen*, brothers and sisters. To be Mapuche is no longer understood as belonging to a global rural proletariat but as being part of a defined ethnic group with its own language, culture, and political struggle to be won.

What brought this change about? In part it was the small but growing number of young people who, rather than simply going into domestic service in Santiago or harvesting grapes in the vineyards, managed to study, to learn about the strange lie that is Chile's history, a history from which they found themselves erased and excluded. In the universities and colleges, in the student dormitories, the youth of the lake came to a new understanding of precisely how and why their rights had been so ignominiously trampled underfoot. Perhaps most importantly, they encountered other young people from those Mapuche communities whose lands had been stolen by the timber and ranching businesses and who had been involved in many decades of struggle to win that land back. And the youth of the lake took these insights back to their parents, their grandparents, their aunts and uncles, in those rural communities once so distant from the places where politics was imagined to happen. This seismic shift in Mapuche politics has gone hand in hand with a shift in how many Mapuche people see themselves. The internalization and stigma of decades of racism has finally started to be overcome by people taking new pride in being Mapuche. And this revalorization of being Mapuche hasn't just occurred among Mapuche people themselves. The recent mass protests across Chile against the ever-rising inequality in access to health, transportation, education, and pensions have frequently aligned themselves with the Mapuche struggle; one has been able to see dozens of *wenufoye* flags being held aloft by young white Chileans at the very heart of white Chilean power. Yet even while the Mapuche political identity has been consolidated, many aspects of Mapuche life continue to be threatened. An old friend, Julio, a teacher of Mapuche language and culture in a rural high school not too far from the lake, explained to me upon my last visit to Chile, "Twenty years ago, all of my students could speak Mapudungun, but they were too ashamed to speak it. Now, they all want to speak it, but they no longer have the words to do so."

This increase in political consciousness has been compelled and accelerated by the spectacular escalation of state violence against Mapuche people. When I still lived at the lake, I remember seeing the spray-painted image of the face of a young man, just a boy really, repeated again and again across the walls of the port, the agricultural towns, and the city: a handsome face with dark eyes, whose

sense of purpose seemed to follow you as you walked past. This was
Alex Lemun, the first Mapuche martyr of the new millennium, shot
dead by police at the age of seventeen as he demanded the return
of his natal land, stolen by a forestry company. Lemun's image was
soon to be replaced by the faces of other young men, the litany of
martyrs growing steadily, the police killing Mapuche with seeming
impunity. The state's response has been to reiterate its designation of
Mapuche activists as brutal "terrorists," at war in a so-called "Mapuche Conflict" and thus subject to Chile's infamous "anti-terrorist"
law, which strips anybody arbitrarily accused of terrorism of their
basic civil rights. To date, this law has only ever been used against
Mapuche people. In pushing for the application of this law, the
police marshaled "evidence" of Mapuche terrorism that they had
supposedly gathered in *Operación Huracán*, "Operation Hurricane,"
an enormous police surveillance operation: huge caches of arms,
burnt-out forestry trucks, and audio recordings of conspiracies. The
bizarre image of these burnt-out trucks with their cargo of highly
flammable (and highly valuable) timber miraculously untouched by
the flames soon raised people's suspicions, and it wasn't long before
the whole thing was revealed as an elaborate setup, constructed in
its entirety by corrupt policemen. Mapuche patience began to wear
thin, and dozens of political prisoners entered into a hunger strike
in protest at the continual erasure of their rights. At heart, the root
issue remains the same as always: land. Mapuche means "people of
the land," and without their land they cease to be truly Mapuche.
The demands for their ancestral right to the land to be recognized
and for their rightful place to be granted them in Chile's constitution
are steps toward restoring and securing the Mapuche people's relationship with the lands that constitute who they are. The election in
2021 of Elisa Loncón, a Mapuche scholar and activist, as president
of the assembly charged with rewriting Chile's constitution would
have been unthinkable twenty-five years earlier; the fact that she gave
her acceptance speech in Mapudungun even more so. Yet the path of

Mapuche politics has been neither smooth nor simple; the progressive constitution put forward by Loncón, proposing Chile as a plurinational state, was rejected in the plebiscite of 2022, and some of the communities most strongly opposed to the proposals were Mapuche communities themselves.

*   *   *

A few years after my initial stay at the lake, I returned, this time with my young family in tow. It would be just a short stay: three months, during which time I would try to lay the groundwork for a book project on the meteoric rise of Pentecostal Christianity in Mapuche communities (a book that, for various reasons, I ultimately abandoned before I had even fully begun it). I had underestimated, or perhaps plain forgotten, just how bleak remote rural homesteads could be in the middle of the harsh southern winter. The drumming of the rain on the tin roofs was a constant background to all conversation, and there was a pervasive, inescapable damp. It was a damp that followed you from room to room, from change of clothes to change of clothes, a damp that penetrated your skin and enveloped your bones with a dull, numbing chill. As winter progressed, people would huddle closer and closer to the wooden stoves, and clothes would soon bear the singe marks of flying sparks. Juan would sometimes fill a low metal tray with smoldering orange embers from the stove and drag it under the kitchen table to warm our legs as we sat drinking *mate* in the evening. More than once, I inadvertently rested my foot on the tray, but in each case was soon alerted by the acrid smell of burning woolen socks and the pain of my burnt feet. Legions of fleas would seek refuge inside houses, getting into the seams of trousers and jackets, populating every fold of bedding. Some kind of allergy to their bites left my body covered from head to toe in huge red welts. And worst of all was the boredom: there really wasn't much of anything to do. The agricultural work that kept people busy for most of the year couldn't take place in the driving rain and knee-deep mud. People stayed indoors, watched TV, and slept.

It was into the bleakness of this kind of winter that I herded my wife, our three-year-old daughter, and our four-year-old son, bringing them to stay at Juan and Marta's house at the side of the lake. Juan was there to meet us off the bus, with his oxcart in tow, the steam rising off the oxen's backs mingling with the winter's fog all around us. The children, born and raised in the city, were simultaneously shocked and enchanted at the very existence of oxen and oxcarts, even more so when it became apparent that they were actually going to ride on the back of the cart! For them at least, the enchantment didn't wear off over those long three months. Their joy at the constant novelties and surprises of rural life remained constant and undiminished: to be greeted every morning by pigs, chickens, dogs, cats, and sheep; to finally encounter in the flesh all of these creatures only previously glimpsed in children's books. They would happily accompany me here and there on my trips around the lake, always prepared in their shiny rubber boots for the thick mud to which the winter rains had reduced every path. They would sit patiently under kitchen tables, playing with kittens, while I talked and attempted to interview people about their sporadic oscillations between Catholic and evangelical iterations of their faith. They took pride in seeing their father play football on waterlogged pitches, despite the heavy defeats and litanies of missed chances. In short, they had that childhood resilience that is rooted in and buoyed up by a perpetual fascination with the world, a fascination that so soon becomes lost to us in adolescence and adulthood.

More than fifteen years later now, there are just two memories that both my children clearly retain from those months: the killing of a pig and the funeral of a woman. The pig was a huge, oversized *huacho* that had been enclosed and carefully nurtured with the tastiest of food scraps over the preceding weeks and months. The hidden connections among life, death, violence, and food were revealed to the children over the course of half an hour, one bitingly cold Saturday morning. They stood in open-mouthed silence as the huge pig was bound and then stabbed through the heart. Their jaws dropped further as pulses of the brightest crimson blood arced through the air onto the mud. And their eyes opened further still as the carcass was butchered, piece by piece. They were both struck mute—the first time they'd ever been lost for words—and I was afraid that they might never recover from this trauma I had inflicted upon them. However, they both soon revived. Marta cut chunks off of the thick layer of precious fat that enveloped the animal just under its skin and placed them in a huge cauldron, hanging under a makeshift roof that had been leaned up against the side of the barn. The fire underneath slowly rendered the fat down, until the cauldron was filled with a viscous, golden liquid. While this process was underway, she had set herself and my wife to peeling countless potatoes and cutting them into fries. With a huge, perforated ladle she extracted the shriveled-up pieces of crispy skin, with its fat now boiled away, the "scratchings" as we used to call them growing up, to accompany our *mate* later in the day. The children's attention was as absolute now as it had been on the pig in its final moments, their eyes fixed on the yellow plastic bowl in which the raw fries lay, a small cup of salt waiting to be scattered over them. A rush of foam and bubbles came to the surface as Marta dumped the fries into the boiling fat, keeping them moving with her ladle. As the children edged closer, she lifted out some of the fries, and then lowered them back in until the required shade of yellowed gold had been reached and a delicate sprinkling of salt applied. These fries were the best thing any of us had ever eaten.

The second memory that has stayed with them is that of the funeral that followed soon after the cold, bright morning when we received the news that Geraldo's wife, Josefina, had finally died. She had been ill for some time and Juan had already told me that her situation was grave. And now she was dead. We would go to her wake and then, the following day, to her funeral. I was deeply fond of Geraldo, one of my many "uncles" at the lake. He was ostracized by many, feared for his rumored expertise in the dark arts, and envied for the relative success of his children, both of them teachers in local schools—but he had always shown me great warmth, and we always seemed to make each other laugh whenever we met. I would occasionally go and visit him and his wife at their small house nestled at the side of one of the lake's many fingerlike inlets. Unlike many rural Mapuche women at that time, so often ground down by the weight of patriarchy, his wife, Josefina, was confident and forthright in her views. When guests arrived, she didn't simply retreat to the kitchen and hide behind the stove but saw herself as a full and equal partner in the life they shared together. I had once happened to turn up in September, the day before the *Fiestas Patrias* celebrating Chilean independence—always celebrated by Mapuche people with a certain irony at feting the root cause of their own oppression—and she'd been frying *empanadas*, little pasties with minced meat, olive, and a piece of boiled egg traditionally eaten at this time. She handed me a plate of them and carefully watched the delight spreading over my face as I bit into the crisp fried dough and let the juices inside it flow freely through my mouth and across my tongue. On that occasion, I stayed talking with them long into the night, and the supply of *empanadas* seemed endless.

But a long, hard illness had reduced her, both physically and socially. She stopped going out, and when people came to visit her, it was evident that her usual vitality was slowly ebbing away. She died just as the moon waned, her strength, love, and productivity deeply rooted in and connected to the world around her until the end. In the afternoon of the day that the news of her death had reached us, my wife and I walked with Juan and Marta through the densely wooded gullies to reach Geraldo's small homestead. We bore sugar, *mate*, and wine to help at the wake and to show our condolences, to give our sadness material form. Geraldo met us at the gate; he was the *ngen lladkun*, "the owner of grief." His deteriorating eyesight meant that his eyes were permanently watery, so nobody could be sure of the cause of the tears that came slipping down his cheeks. We entered a room full of people all seated against the walls of a small room, thus encircling the body laid out in the middle. They all knew me, but none of them knew my wife, and so they were torn between the obligation to greet a newcomer and the need to maintain a doleful respect for the dead. But Geraldo knew what to do. He gently guided us to a corner but took the long way around his wife's body, thus giving people the chance to greet us without having to leave their spots on the rough-hewn bench. A bottle of wine was placed in front of us, and as we drank, our attention rested on the corpse laid out on the table in front of us. The room seemed more brightly lit than at most wakes I'd been to, and in that bright light, Josefina's face seemed sharper, more angular than I could remember it being in life. Perhaps somebody had made an attempt at applying makeup: some blusher to her cheeks, lipstick to her mouth. I felt stretched and confused. Excited to be there with my wife after a few years away, but confused and dismayed that a person I once knew as living was now dead, stunned again by the awfulness of human mortality. Over the years, the dead I have seen have accumulated in my mind, but that initial shock, the dissonance between the memory of the living person and the brutal reality of a corpse, doesn't seem to diminish at all.

We didn't stay that long at the wake. As members of the extended kin group and community—the *lof*—of which Josefina had been a part, Juan and Marta would be obliged to provide food and drink for the many guests who would arrive at her funeral the next day. This would mean an early start for Juan to kill and butcher yet another pig, and an even earlier one for Marta to get the first bus to the port to buy supplies. So, guided by the dim light of the tiny flashlight attached to my key ring, we stumbled back through the woods and gullies toward home, where our children lay sleeping, looked after by Juan and Marta's own children, themselves now parents as well.

It's often said by Mapuche people that the weather at a funeral will match the character of the deceased: mourners at the funeral of

a person with a stormy, violent temperament will doubtless be battered by thunder and lightning, while those at the funeral of somebody who lived at peace with others will enjoy a calm, bright day.
The idea that weather reflects human life is sometimes dismissed in
the Western tradition as a "pathetic fallacy," but from the perspective
of people for whom there is no radical separation between the world
and human life, such an idea is anything but fallacious—if we are
part of the world, truly intrinsic to it and it to us, how could it remain
indifferent to our passing? The sky was the deepest blue as we set out
with the oxcart to take the road that looped the long way around the
lake's various incursions, to a field near Geraldo's house where the
funeral was to take place. We had a butchered pig, several carafes of
wine, a huge mound of firewood, a table and two benches, and several children all balancing on the back of the cart. Although it was
winter, the birds were singing with the vigor of spring.

Most of the other families of the community had already set up
their cooking fires, tables, and chairs around the outer edges of the
small field by the time we got there, and the initial trickle of guests
from neighboring communities had started to arrive and be invited
to one of the tables. We helped Juan and Marta set up their outdoor
kitchen, got the fire going to roast the large slabs of raw meat, and
decanted wine from the plastic carafes into glass bottles to be given
to each guest. By the time Juan was in a position to start beckoning
his friends over from among the milling guests, the small field had
filled with people. It was at this moment that Marta lifted her head
from the heavily smoking fire and asked, "Where are the children?"
They had, as toddlers do, toddled off. I skirted the field, pausing at
each table to see if they'd maybe snuck underneath one of them to
try and pilfer the disks of bread fried in pork fat for which they'd
developed a real passion, but there was no sign of them anywhere.
Finally, turning back toward the far side of the field, I spotted two
garish pairs of rubber boots attached to muddy bodies in the middle
of the muddy field. It was my turn to drop my jaw as I saw my son,

the elder of the two, hoist his sister up so that she could get a good look at Josefina's body in the open casket. As she clung to the side of the coffin, trying to haul herself up, with her brother behind her, heaving her upward with all his force, I had a horrific vision of the entire coffin tipping off its flimsy stand and emptying its contents prematurely into the wet earth. I couldn't shout, for fear of drawing everyone's attention to this impending calamity, nor did I feel that I could sprint across the sober field, so I tried a kind of goose-stepping speed walk. But I'd barely advanced five yards before I was stopped. Tomás stepped in front of me with an outstretched bottle of wine and a glass. To refuse a glass of wine at a funeral was beyond the pale, so I took the glass and smiled weakly. But as I gulped down the sweet red wine, my eyes frantically scanned the scene behind Tomás, two yellow boots kicking the air as my daughter successfully hauled herself up the side of the coffin. I handed the empty glass back to Tomás and raced toward the coffin. The children had once again found themselves lost for words in the face of death, peering over the edge at Josefina's flower-covered corpse. I gently lifted my daughter off the coffin and led her and her brother quietly back toward Juan and Marta's table. My eyes were fixed on the ground as we walked, not wanting to know if anybody had seen us, not wanting my face to burn still further with shame. I made the children sit on the back of the oxcart, but not before my daughter, having noticed the strange, oft-noted effect of death on Josefina's face, raised her head and asked, "Why did the dead lady have a mustache?" The fact that nobody around could hear us, or even spoke English, was of little consolation. I was angry: not at my daughter, but at the sheer and utter indignity wrought by death, that somebody so strong could be so reduced. Yet at the same time, I knew that Josefina would not have seen it this way; she would have laughed with the little girl, laughed at herself, smiled at the very nature of a world of which she was a cherished part.

*   *   *

So I'd left the lake, returned home, married, had children, gotten a job, and moved to a new city. I would return to the lake every couple of years to visit friends for a week or two, happy to see them, content and secure of my place in the world. I took the things I'd learned there and transformed them into the usual commodities of academic life: lectures, books, essays. Life progressed. Then, there came a morning when I reached my office, turned on the computer, opened my email, and was confronted by a message accusing me, in glaring block capitals, of stealing secret knowledge and selling Mapuche ritual secrets.

The message had been sent to dozens of people, including many of the most powerful and influential in my field. I swelled up immediately with self-righteous anger and responded without hesitation, pointing out my accuser's false claims of authority, his lack of standing in the community, his own flaws and misdeeds, and in all of these comments, my anger congealed and took aim, framed to inflict damage and cause pain. All hell broke loose. Various message boards and forums filled with opinions, some for me, most against. The community where I'd lived at the lake produced a statement of support for me that was more or less completely ignored, the voices of the very people I was supposed to have hurt apparently being, ironically, the ones that mattered least.

It was very easy to be angry, and even easier to feel wronged, to lament the grave injustice of it all and wrap myself in the comforting blanket of victimhood. And in all of this anger, all of this lamentation, it never occurred to me to pause and consider that there might have been some truth in what my accuser had said: perhaps not the exact kind of truth that he had intended, but an accidental truth, somehow revealing something that, deep down, I already knew. It took years for this possibility to finally dawn upon me. Although I had neither been a member of the CIA nor ever stolen anybody's "secret knowledge," I had indeed stolen something. I had stolen my friends' land, their livelihoods, their culture, their language, their dignity, and their lives. Willingly or not, I had become an intrinsic part of that global system of resource extraction sometimes called colonialism, sometimes called capitalism, that had reduced and degraded the Mapuche in so many ways. I'd somehow imagined that my scholarly critiques of this colonialist and capitalist system insulated me from it, made me exempt from criticism, detached and immune. But even those critiques were, I had to eventually recognize, a part of the very system against which they were directed, built as they were upon difference, objectification, and the strange perpetually deferred promise of the other. My greatest failure, then, was simply not seeing: not seeing who I was, and not seeing that I, too, had been complicit all along.

I didn't grow from this failure, I shrank. I slowly came to realize that, for me at least, the anthropological project—its asymmetry, its objectification, and its violence—had to be given up. It was a discipline that was, despite its own frenzied protestations, inevitably trapped in an endlessly repeating drama of failed escape from the political conditions that made it possible in the first place. It had to be given up, and for many years, that is what I did: I gave up. I pottered around the edges of academic life and, eventually, started a new collaborative research project on the other side of the world.

As time went by, however, I noticed a subtle, almost incremental change. I was receiving more and more requests to review articles by Mapuche anthropologists or to examine their masters' or doctoral theses. To my surprise, more and more Mapuche people seemed to be salvaging something of value from anthropology, but it certainly wasn't the model of Susan Sontag's heroic anthropologist, venturing into strange and exotic realms to bring back the myriad potential of humanity for a disillusioned West. The anthropology that they sought was, instead, one that would allow them to understand what was happening to their own communities: to understand both the machinations of colonial power and the deeply wrought connections with the world that had allowed the Mapuche to successfully resist those attempts to destroy, usurp, and commodify their land. The understandings of these processes could then be transformed, not into tired academic publications but into action: expert witness statements in court hearings, media appearances, legal complaints. And it was not only their anthropological focus that was different; their way of doing anthropology also differed. These new researchers did not rely on the productive frictions of failure but followed, instead, their culturally established pathways of understanding, seeking knowledge from their kin and elders, understanding that this knowledge could never be completely stripped from the land beneath their feet and the stars above their heads. Anthropology then, was not abandoned but transformed.

Last year, I was sitting drinking *mate* tea with a Mapuche friend at his home not far from the regional capital. He had recently completed his PhD in anthropology at a university outside of Chile, and I had been the examiner of his thesis. I was whining yet again about my disappointment that certain Mapuche people had not spoken out publicly on my behalf when I was faced with those accusations, ten years previously. He interrupted me, laughing: "Look, we knew that you were right and he was wrong, but that's completely irrelevant; after five hundred years of oppression, we're never going to support the white guy over the Mapuche guy!" With this lighthearted admonishment from my friend, my eyes were finally opened to the fact that my own actions and intentions could not be quarantined, could not be extricated from the structures of inequality that had allowed me to move to the lake in the first place. For I had been the witch, the clown, and the usurper all at once and all along, seeking to destroy, failing to understand, and turning into property those things that can never be owned. I won't say that I've grown from these failures; I've surely repeated many of them. But I have perhaps become better able to understand how and why the key qualities that failure reveals—strength, generosity, clarity, and wisdom—underpin the love and respect that mark the true person and toward which we all must strive.

A Guide to Further Reading

The reader will have noticed that this book contains none of the usual academic citations. The reason for this omission is twofold: first, so as not to disrupt the flow of the stories themselves, and second, because many of the ideas presented here come from the voices of my friends at the lake. I feared that juxtaposing those with standard academic citations would risk introducing a hierarchy in which the written word—and especially the word written in English—would always win out, the oral being relegated to nothing more than fuel for a literary fire. A truly decolonial anthropology (and I am under no illusion that the present text is a part of that) will need to include a more direct and forceful confrontation with the linguistic forms and registers it takes. All of that said, however, this book, being an account of my own personal and intellectual trajectory, inevitably bears the traces of all the texts I've read over the years. What follows is not at all intended to be comprehensive, but rather to offer the interested reader a few key starting points for exploring further some of the issues discussed and, perhaps, for gaining a clearer idea of how my own thinking has been shaped.

In terms of its narrative form and style, this book was inspired by a long tradition of anthropological memoir and auto-ethnography. This trend has many genealogies, but particularly salient is a feminist one that goes back to the works of Zora Neale Hurston and has been taken forward by anthropologists like Lila Abu-Lughod, Ruth Behar, Kirin Narayan, Margery Wolf, and, most recently, Clara Han in her book *Seeing Like a Child*. A different genealogy of anthropological memoir can be located in the specific context of South America, where Lévi-Strauss's *Tristes Tropiques* remains essential, Pierre Clastres's *Chronicles of the Guayaki Indians* and Philippe Descola's *Spears of Twilight* are intriguing contributions, and Aparecida Vilaça's *Paletó and Me* is a recent gem. Debates about the complex politics of ethnographic writing are so numerous that they have almost generated a subdiscipline in their own right, with James Clifford and George Marcus's *Writing Culture* remaining a key touchstone. A recent contribution worth exploring is Anand Pandian and Stuart McLean's edited volume on experimental ethnography, *Crumpled Paper Boat*.

These debates about the writing of anthropology cannot be detached from the politics of anthropology and, in particular, its attempts to purge itself of its inherent coloniality. The present book is intended not as a contribution to this goal but, rather, an account of my own personal, and embarrassingly tardy, realization of why such a goal is necessary. Again, one could trace any number of genealogies of this critique, but key texts include Talal Asad's *Anthropology and the Colonial Encounter* and Faye Harrison's *Decolonizing Anthropology*. Whether anthropology has a future or not remains something of an open question, with those responding to it covering a wide range—from those like Ryan Cecil Jobson who think the entire field should be left to burn, to those who see the possibility of a positive repurposing, exemplified by the volume *Decolonizing Ethnography* by Carolina Alonso Bejarano, Lucia López Juárez, Mirian Mijangos García, and Daniel Goldstein. Yet it is perhaps significant that most of the Mapuche anthropologists I know have very little interest in these debates, which they consider to be quite parochial, restricted to the elite and increasingly irrelevant academic centers of power in Europe and North America. Their concern is less with the discipline of anthropology per se than with the utility of anthropological methods for their own struggles to assert the validity of Mapuche lifeways in an increasingly hostile Chilean context.

Moving from the failures of anthropology to failure more generally, we find that most writing on the topic is, well, a failure, in that it portrays it as simply an inconvenient yet necessary step towards success. An exception to this trope, and by far the best book I've read on the subject, is Joe Moran's *If You Should Fail*.

The body of writing about Mapuche lives is too vast for me to trace anything but its outlines here. It is perhaps useful to distinguish between those texts written *about* Mapuche people and those written *by* Mapuche people. Writing by *winka* about Mapuche goes back several hundred years, to the early missionary texts, such as that by Diego de Rosales. What could be called the "modern" era of anthropological writing about Mapuche society was initiated by writers like Louis Faron, Ines Hilger, Mischa Titiev, Thomas Melville, and Milan Stuchlik in the mid-twentieth century. More recent anthropological accounts include those by Cristóbal Bonelli on health and healing, Ana Mariella Bacigalupo on shamanism, Tom Dillehay on landscape and archaeology, Rolf Foerster and Helmut Schindler on religion, Marcelo González on identity, and Piergiorgio Di Giminiani on land rights, Anne Lavanchy on gender and migration, to name but a few. Historians like José Bengoa, Joana Crow, and Florencia Mallon have also made valuable contributions to understanding the twentieth-century trajectory of Mapuche society. Writings by Mapuche people about Mapuche society are again too numerous for me to do anything other than scrape the surface of them here. A key early text is Pascual Coña's *Testimonio de un Cacique Mapuche*, although how much of his original voice was filtered out by the Capuchin missionary who wrote it down is an open question. Manuel Manquilef, Martín Alonqueo, and Juan Ñanculef all produced valuable accounts over the course of the twentieth century, while important recent contributions from this century include works by Pablo Mariman, Pedro Cayuqueo, Ana Millaleo, Sergio Caniuqueo, Elisa Loncón, Enrique Antileo, José Kidel, Rosamel Millaman, and Fernando Pairican, to name but a few.

The most interesting things I've read recently on Mapuche society have all been PhD theses: on museum repatriation and Mapuche theories of objects, by the Brazilian anthropologist Lucas da Costa Maciel; on the Mapuche struggle against petrochemical plants, by the Afro-Brazilian anthropologist Karine Narahara; and on Mapuche ritual, by the Mapuche anthropologist and leader José Kidel. It's interesting to note that none of these correspond to the old model of the solitary anthropologist but, rather, take collaboration and coproduction as axiomatic to the anthropological endeavor. Maybe there is hope for anthropology yet.

Acknowledgments

'm very grateful to Lucas da Costa Maciel, Girish Daswani, Maya Mayblin, Shari Sabeti, Farley Urmston, and Harry Walker for reading and offering advice on earlier drafts of this book. Helen Bleck offered valuable editorial advice on an earlier draft. I am especially grateful to both Delwar Hussain and Fraser MacDonald for their reading and support from a very early stage of writing. Without their encouragement, I would have given up the project long ago. Neither José Kidel, Casey High, nor Arthur Bradford ever read the manuscript, but they each in their own way encouraged me over many years to write these stories down, for which I thank them. My wife, Maya Mayblin, not only read the manuscript but also gave me the support I needed to get it published. Maya and my children, Ezra and Willa, accompanied me to the lake on later visits with an openness and boundless energy that astounds me still. I would also like to acknowledge my mother's unfailing support, from my very first day in Chile all those years ago to the present. I'm grateful to Elisabeth Maselli, Lily Palladino, and to the two anonymous reviewers for the University of Pennsylvania Press for their advice, support, and enthusiasm for the project.

I hope that it's obvious from these pages just how much I owe to my friends at the lake. For a variety of reasons, I won't name them all individually, but they know who they are and what they mean to me. Even if this book only conveys a small fraction of what they taught me about trying to live a better life, it will have been worth the effort.

www.ingramcontent.com/pod-product-compliance
Lightning Source LLC
Chambersburg PA
CBHW032351280326
41935CB00008B/535